Centerville Library
Washington-Centerville Public Library
Centerville, Ohio
DISCARD

W9-AHN-399

A **BAKER'S FIELD GUIDE** TO

Doughnuts

More Than 60 Warm and Fresh Homemade Treats

DEDE WILSON

THE HARVARD COMMON PRESS

Boston, Massachusetts

THE HARVARD COMMON PRESS
535 Albany Street
Boston, Massachusetts 02118
www.harvardcommonpress.com

Copyright © 2012 by Dede Wilson
Photographs copyright © 2012 by Joyce Oudkerk-Pool

All rights reserved. No part of this publication may be reproduced or transmitted in any form or by any means, electronic or mechanical, including photocopying, recording, or any information storage or retrieval system, without permission in writing from the publisher.

Printed in China
Printed on acid-free paper

Library of Congress Cataloging-in-Publication Data
Wilson, Dede.
  A Baker's field guide to doughnuts : more than 60 warm and fresh homemade treats / Dede Wilson.
    p. cm.
  ISBN 978-1-55832-788-7 (pbk. : acid-free paper)
1. Doughnuts. I. Title. II. Title: Doughnuts.
  TX770.D67W55 2012
  641.81'5—dc23

                                        2012004602

Special bulk-order discounts are available on this and other Harvard Common Press books. Companies and organizations may purchase books for premiums or resale, or may arrange a custom edition, by contacting the Marketing Director at the address above.

Book design by Night & Day Design
Photographs by Joyce Oudkerk-Pool
Author photograph by David Kilroy

10 9 8 7 6 5 4 3 2 1

To my kids—daughter, Ravenna, and sons,

Freeman and Forrester—who all share my

fondness for the kitchen and the table.

And to my fans who keep me going.

Come visit me at dedewilson.com and

let me know what you are baking.

Contents

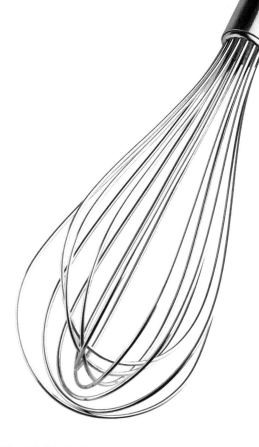

Acknowledgments

Thank you to the Harvard Common Press crew for coming up with the perfect topic for the fifth Baker's Field Guide.

Hugs and kisses, as always, to agents Maureen and Eric Lasher, who treat me like family.

Also a huge nod to Pam Hoenig, who launched the Baker's Field Guide series years ago. Working with her again feels like a comforting full circle.

Introduction

Doughnuts or donuts, however you spell this sweet treat—the mere word elicits a passionate response from devotees. *A Baker's Field Guide to Doughnuts* brings you the recipes and information you need to make airy, yeast-risen doughnuts as well as cakelike baking powder doughnuts in flavors sure to please both kids and adults, whether you're looking for a classic or something new. You will also find doughnuts' brethren, such as fritters, churros, and beignets, in all sorts of flavors, shapes, and sizes.

Doughnut history is murky: Some say they were brought to North America by Dutch settlers, while others point to the fact that archaeologists have found remnants of fried ring-shaped cakes in the southwestern United States, suggesting that they were made by early Native Americans. Regardless of their origin, by the 1920s doughnuts were being mass-produced in the United States and had become a standard American treat. The popularity of doughnuts was firmly cemented with the opening of large chains such as Krispy Kreme and Dunkin' Donuts in the '40s and '50s—in fact, most people have only ever bought their doughnuts, never made them at home.

I hope to change that in *A Baker's Field Guide to Doughnuts,* as making your own doughnuts requires mastering just a few techniques and will reward you with incredible flavor and texture that you simply won't find in store-bought doughnuts.

How to Use This Book

This book accompanies *A Baker's Field Guide to Christmas Cookies*, *A Baker's Field Guide to Chocolate Chip Cookies*, *A Baker's Field Guide to Holiday Candy & Confections*, and *A Baker's Field Guide to Cupcakes*. All of these books feature a user-friendly format in which each recipe—in this case, a doughnut—is presented on its own two-page spread. For each doughnut recipe you will find a Description, Field Notes (extra information about the doughnut), Yield (how many doughnuts the recipes makes), and Lifespan (how long the doughnut will stay fresh and how to store it). You will also find symbols for special characteristics, as listed in the following chart:

KEY TO SYMBOLS

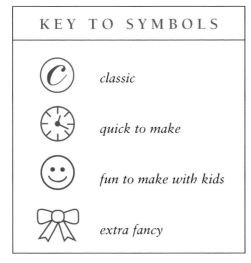

classic

quick to make

fun to make with kids

extra fancy

In the Master Recipes section, you will find the recipes for the basic doughs, glazes, frostings, toppings, and fillings used throughout the book. Master these simple recipes and you've got the building blocks for many of the doughnut recipes presented in the Field Guide section. You can even use them to come up with your own flavor combinations—see Combos to Consider on pages 27 and 33 for a few ideas to get you started.

Ingredients

Here is a short list of ingredients that are frequently called for in this book. If you start with high-quality ingredients, you'll get better results.

BUTTER: Use fresh unsalted butter.

SUGAR: When a recipe simply calls for sugar, it means regular granulated sugar.

Light and dark brown sugar: These should be firmly packed into exact-size measuring cups.

Confectioners' sugar: Also called powdered sugar, this should be sifted before measuring.

Colored sugars, sprinkles/jimmies, and sugar decorations: Whether they are the tiny balls called nonpareils or shaped like bits of confetti, look to cake-decorating supply sources for a variety of choices to enhance your doughnuts.

EGGS: Use eggs graded "large."

FLOUR: Various flours are called for in this book; please use the flours suggested. For all-purpose flour, I use King Arthur Unbleached All-Purpose Flour. For cake flour, I use Softasilk.

LEAVENERS

Baking soda and baking powder: Make sure they are fresh. I use double-acting baking powder.

Yeast: I prefer Red Star active dry yeast. Instant yeast can lessen rising time by as much as 50 percent; feel free to try it in these recipes. In any event, always use yeast before the "best if used by" date.

Proofing Yeast

The instructions in these recipes are specific to Red Star active dry yeast. If you substitute another brand, you should check that company's recommendations for proofing. Use a thermometer to test your water, which should be between 110° and 115°F, then follow the specific instructions in the recipe. If your water is too cool, your doughnuts will have a very slow rise and might never reach their full potential. If your water is too hot, you will kill the yeast. Always use a thermometer and do not rely on touch alone.

Salt: Use table salt, as coarse and kosher salts measure differently.

Milk, cream cheese, sour cream: Use full-fat varieties.

Heavy cream: Use cream labeled "heavy" as opposed to "whipping" for best results. Heavy cream has a higher butterfat content.

Extracts: Use pure vanilla and almond extracts, not those containing artificial flavors.

Citrus zests: Make sure to use just the colored part of the zest and not the bitter white pith that lies beneath. Use a Microplane zester for best results.

Chocolate

Bittersweet and semisweet chocolate: While these chocolates can be used interchangeably with fairly reliable results, if I specify a particular chocolate, I suggest using it for best results. For supermarket brands I use Ghirardelli, found in the bakery aisle, or Callebaut, which can often be bought in bulk. For specialty chocolates I like Valrhona and Scharffen Berger.

Milk chocolate: I recommend Callebaut, Scharffen Berger, Ghirardelli, or Valrhona.

White chocolate: Look for white chocolate that lists cocoa butter in the ingredients and not palm or other oils. The cocoa butter will give it a chocolatey flavor and aroma. I most often use Callebaut and Valrhona.

Unsweetened cocoa powder: Some of the recipes call for Dutch-processed cocoa powder, while others require natural cocoa powder. Check the label—it might say "Dutch," "Dutched," or "alkalized," but if it says "natural" (or nothing at all), that's the other kind. They cannot be used interchangeably.

Nuts: Make sure the nuts you use are fresh, with no rancid smell. Store nuts in the refrigerator or freezer in airtight containers.

Toasting Nuts

Spread the nuts in a single layer on a rimmed baking sheet pan and toast in a preheated 350°F oven until fragrant and just beginning to color. Toss them around once or twice during toasting.

Baking time will vary depending on the quantity of nuts on the pan as well as the type of nut. Always cool nuts before chopping or grinding. The oils, which will have been brought to the surface by the heat, must be reabsorbed or the nuts could turn greasy when chopped.

Coconut: I call for two different coconut products in this book. One is 100 percent unsweetened coconut milk, which can be found in the Asian section of most large supermarkets or in Asian food stores. Make sure it is not cream of coconut, which is highly sweetened and typically used for piña coladas. The other product called for is sweetened long-shred coconut, which you can find in any supermarket baking aisle.

Spices: All of the spices in this book are ground unless otherwise indicated.

Make sure your spices are not stale—if a spice jar has been on your shelf for longer than six months, it's time to replace it.

OIL AND FRYING FATS: Most of these doughnuts are fried, and your choice of fat can make a difference. The choice of liquid oil, lard, or shortening is a personal preference. I like canola oil for the balance it presents between neutral flavor, cost, and availability. Whatever fat you use, make sure it is deep enough to truly deep-fry the doughnuts. Also, make sure it is clean, and do not reuse it too many times. I usually change the fat after frying two or three batches of doughnuts. Of course, use your eyes and nose as well. If the oil has a lot of suspended particles from bits of dough or if it smells off, by all means change it. (For more in-depth information, see Choosing Your Frying Fat on page 14.)

Equipment

PASTRY BAG, COUPLER, AND TIPS: Some of these recipes require the use of a pastry bag and decorating tips. Where the directions call for a pastry bag and coupler and a specific tip, this means that the tip requires a coupler to be used. When a coupler is not suggested, it is intended that you insert the tip, in this case a larger one, such as Ateco #847 for Churros (page 88), directly into the pastry bag. For filling doughnuts with jelly, jam, or custard, I recommend an Ateco #230 Bismarck tip. This tip has a sharp, slanted opening, perfect for inserting into doughnuts and creating a channel for your filling.

DEEP-FAT FRYER: This electric appliance makes deep-frying easy and keeps the kitchen clean. I rely on my Waring Pro deep-fat fryer. With 1800 watts, it makes perfect doughnuts as well as French fries and tempura. Set the thermostat and in just a few minutes, you are ready to fry.

HEAVY, DEEP POT: If you are not using an electric deep-fat fryer, then you need a sturdy, heavy pot deep enough to hold at least 3 inches of fat with plenty of clearance and wide enough to hold at least three doughnuts at a time without crowding. Cast iron or enamel-coated cast iron is great, as are triple-ply stainless-steel or anodized aluminum pots.

THERMOMETER: An accurate thermometer is helpful for assessing water temperature when proofing yeast and oil temperature during frying. I recommend the Maverick CT-03 digital oil and candy thermometer. You can set it for your desired temperature and it beeps to tell you when the temperature has been reached. It easily attaches to most pots with an adjustable clip.

MEASURING CUPS AND SPOONS: For dry ingredients, I use high-quality stainless-steel cups and spoons that are sturdy enough not to dent (dents make for inaccurate measurements), such as those made by Cuisipro. I use the dip and sweep method for measuring sugar and flour. Whisk the flour first to aerate it, then dip and sweep the top even with the back of a knife.

For liquid measurements, I use the standard Pyrex measuring cups available at most supermarkets and kitchenware stores. Always try to use a cup similar to the amount you are measuring—in other words, do not use a 4-cup measuring cup to measure out ½ cup of liquid.

ELECTRIC MIXER: I used a freestanding 5-quart KitchenAid mixer to test these recipes. If you are using a hand-held mixer, the mixing times will be longer.

FOOD PROCESSOR: These recipes were tested with a Cuisinart Elite 12-cup food processor.

MICROWAVE OVEN: I use the microwave to melt dark chocolate and butter. It is hard to standardize recipes using microwave ovens, as they come equipped with various wattages. Always follow your manufacturer's directions for specific information. Start by microwaving on 30 percent power for short periods of time.

JELLYROLL PANS/RIMMED BAKING SHEET PANS: These recipes were tested with heavyweight aluminum or stainless-steel rimmed sheet pans, which I refer to as rimmed baking sheet pans.

DOUGHNUT CUTTERS: The classic doughnut shape—a ring with a hole cut out of the center—can be made with one specialized cutter. I use a Johnson-Rose 3-inch cutter for my ring-shaped doughnuts. It is very sturdy and will last a lifetime; it is easily found online at Amazon and elsewhere. Alternatively, you can use a plain round cutter 3 inches in diameter and then a 1-inch cutter for the center hole. If you are making round doughnuts without a center hole (as for Jelly Doughnuts, page 124), then just use a plain round 2½-inch cutter, either purchased alone or as part of a set of plain round cutters. The 2½-inch size is perfect for filled doughnuts—any larger and they become floppy and unwieldy, and the ratio of dough to filling is not optimal.

DOUGHNUT PANS: A few recipes use doughnut pans, which have doughnut-shaped wells in which to place your batter/dough. They are meant to hold softer doughs. The ones I use are manufactured by

Norpro and come in standard (3½-inch) and mini (2-inch) sizes. They can be found at King Arthur Flour (see Resources, page 173).

Time to Make the Doughnuts

This section provides you with all of the background information you need to make doughnuts, from forming to filling, frying to glazing, and everything in between. Read this section thoroughly at least once and refer to the Doughnut Troubleshooting section (page 17) as needed.

Forming Doughnuts

Most of the doughs in this book are rolled out to a ½-inch thickness (follow the specific directions in each recipe). Just as with pie dough, you will need a lightly floured work surface (unless otherwise indicated) and aim to handle the dough lightly, so as to retain the best texture. Simply scrape the dough onto the surface, gently pat it down, and apply light pressure with a rolling pin. I recommend that you use a ruler to measure the desired thickness of the dough as opposed to attempting this by eye. After your initial cuts with a floured cutter, gently gather the dough, reroll, and cut again. Try not to roll out the dough a third time, or you might end up with tough doughnuts.

Filling Doughnuts Before Frying

Believe it or not, you can fill doughnuts before frying them, and sometimes it is preferable to take this approach. I like to fill prior to frying when the filling is very sticky (like Nutella), which can be

Doughnut Do-Ahead

For yeast-raised doughnuts, there are points in the recipes when the dough needs to rest and rise. Take advantage of these long pauses to make your topping or glaze, prepare your paper towel–lined pan, or set up your frying station.

For cake-style doughnuts, most doughs need to spend at least 1 hour in the refrigerator, but they can chill for longer. The doughs usually come together very quickly; consider making them in the evening and putting them in the refrigerator overnight—then, in the morning, the rolling and cutting will go swiftly. If your dough has chilled for more than an hour or two, however, it will be too cold to go directly into the hot oil. After cutting, let the doughnuts sit at room temperature until just barely chilled, usually around 10 to 15 minutes, depending on room temperature. But be careful not let them warm up too much or they will lose their shape when you pick them up.

difficult to pipe afterward; when there is more than one filling (such as PB&J); and also when the filling is too chunky to flow through a pastry tip (as when using a chunky fruit preserve). Roll the risen yeast dough out to a ¼-inch thickness and cut into an even number of 2½-inch rounds. Dollop the filling in the centers of half of the rounds. Brush the edges of the filled rounds with water. Top with the other rounds and seal the edges well by firmly pressing every part of the edge with your fingers. Let rise a second time. After the rising, the seam will be invisible. It's like magic!

Choosing Your Frying Fat

You have choices when it comes to the fat used for frying doughnuts. Canola oil, safflower oil, sunflower oil, and grape-seed oil all have high smoke points (so they remain stable at high temperatures), making them good for high-temperature frying. Corn oil and peanut oil are also good for frying but can impart flavors to the doughnuts—of course, for Peanut Butter–Glazed Jelly Doughnuts (page 136), peanut oil would fit the bill. Lard has been a favored frying medium of choice for decades, and some folks main-tain that you can't achieve that unique doughnut quality without it. Solid veg-etable shortening can be used as well, although it has fallen out of favor due to health concerns over hydrogenated fats. On the plus side, devotees of fried foods say that doughnuts fried in vegetable shortening have a less greasy exterior and are drier to the touch. It's your choice. Whatever fat you use, it will degrade with multiple uses. I use fresh fat for each new recipe. Also, if you are using an electric fryer, follow the manufac-turer's instructions regarding what types of fat to use; many caution against using solid fats.

Frying Doughnuts

Most of the doughnuts in this book are fried. You can fry in an electric deep-fat fryer or in a heavy, deep pot, measuring the heat of the oil with a thermometer. The fat should be at least 3 inches deep (with a couple of inches of headroom so that you don't get splattered), and the diameter of the vessel should be large enough to hold at least three doughnuts at a time.

Once you have chosen your frying equipment, set up your work area. Next to your fryer place two rimmed baking sheet pans lined with three layers of absorbent paper towels. If you have a rack that fits in the pan, place that down first and the towels on top of that.

Make sure that all of your doughnuts are free of excess flour before frying. If there is excess flour, use a soft, dry pastry brush to brush it off. I sometimes pick up cake-style doughnuts with my fingers and slip them into the oil. This technique works best with sturdy doughs that keep their shape. (You will be able to tell when you attempt to pick one up.) Alternatively, you can use a metal spatula with a heatproof handle and a thin, sharp edge. Another technique to try (this works best for yeast-risen doughnuts) is to first dip the spatula into the hot oil and then lift up a doughnut with it. Then carefully lower the spatula with the doughnut into the oil and jiggle the spatula until the doughnut floats off into the oil. It is also a good idea to have a wooden chopstick handy to flip the doughnuts over in the oil halfway through cooking, and a metal skimmer or slotted spoon to remove the doughnuts from the hot fat.

Each recipe suggests a frying temperature, and I suggest you fry a test doughnut at that temperature. If your ingredients are colder than mine, you might need a slightly lower temperature for your doughnuts to cook through before getting too brown on the outside. Or, if you make your doughnuts much larger or smaller, the temperature, and certainly the frying time, will vary. Typically, doughnuts are best fried between 350° and 365°F. While this temperature range may seem fairly small, micro-adjustments will make a big difference, so turn your heat up or down accordingly. I give a 5-degree range within each recipe because it is very hard to keep oil at a constant temperature if you are frying on the stovetop. If you have an electric fryer, set the temperature in the middle of the given range. The aim is to create a golden brown exterior and a just-cooked interior.

Doughnuts will become dry if overfried. With very dark doughnuts, such as chocolate, it is difficult to gauge doneness by color. In these cases, pay special attention to the time cues; frying a test doughnut is very helpful. **Even fifteen seconds can mean the difference between undercooked, perfect, and overcooked.**

Once the doughnuts are removed from the oil and placed on paper towels to drain, wait about 10 seconds, then flip them over to a clean area of paper towel to drain on the other side. If your doughnut is going to be coated with confectioners' sugar, cinnamon sugar, or the like, have those ready at hand, as the doughnuts should be coated while warm. Glazes can typically be applied to cooled but still warm doughnuts. Cool doughnuts completely before filling with custards or dairy-based fillings for food safety reasons.

What About the Holes?

Doughnut holes are, of course, the round center pieces of dough that are left over after you have cut out your doughnut rings. Some folks love them, but I think the ratio of crusty exterior to softer interior is not optimal compared to that of an actual doughnut. Instead, I choose to roll out the holes along with all of the other dough scraps and cut out as many more true doughnuts as possible. When I want to make doughnut holes, I use a 1½-inch round cutter for all of the dough. Any doughnut dough can be cut out as holes; simply fry them for a shorter period of time.

Baking Doughnuts

I like to use doughnut pans for baked doughnuts, as they help give the finished doughnut a pleasantly rounded shape. Look for Norpro Nonstick Donut Pans (see Resources, page 173) in both standard and mini sizes. The baked doughnuts in this book use the standard size, but you could use the same recipes for the mini pans and just adjust the baking time.

Filling Doughnuts After Frying

The jelly doughnut and the buttercream doughnut are the classics of the filled doughnut genre. A long, narrow pastry tip, called a Bismarck tip, is used to facilitate the process of filling doughnuts. The tip is fitted into a pastry bag, which is filled halfway with the filling of choice, and then the tip is inserted halfway into the cooked and completely cooled doughnut. For light, airy doughnuts, all you have to do is apply pressure to the bag and the filling will flow freely into the doughnut. Continue to apply pressure as you withdraw the tip. For dense dough-nuts, insert the tip, wiggle it around in a circular motion to create an air pocket, then squeeze the bag to insert the filling. You can also poke to the left, jiggle, insert filling, remove the tip partially, poke to the right, jiggle, and insert filling again.

Glazing and Frosting Doughnuts

A simple sugar glaze can subtly enhance the inherent yeasty qualities of a raised doughnut—or dominate in the case of a chocolate glaze. Some glazes are dry to the touch and crackle between your teeth, while others stay alluringly soft and sticky. I think both types have their place, and both are represented in this book. With either type, the doughnuts require a nice dunking in the glaze. This is best accomplished by making the glaze right before you are going to use it and placing it in a bowl that is wide enough to accommodate the doughnut's width, along with room for your fingers. Take one barely warm doughnut at a time, hold it by its sides, and dip a broad side of it into the glaze. Press it gently into the glaze so that it comes at least halfway up the sides of the doughnut. Gently rotate the doughnut as you remove it from the glaze, flipping it upright and placing it on a rack or baking sheet to dry. Both firm and soft glazes will improve from a brief rest. They will lose some of their stickiness, making them more pleasant to handle and eat. If the glaze starts setting up in the bowl while you are still working with it, simply whisk it until smooth or reheat it. You can also apply a glaze by spooning it over the doughnuts with a cereal spoon or spreading it with a small offset spatula. The offset spatula is also the tool of choice for spreading frosting on top of doughnuts, as with Cream Cheese Frosting (page 41).

Applying Dry Coatings

Cinnamon sugar–coated doughnuts and confectioners' sugar–coated (powdered) doughnuts are two classics found in every doughnut shop. These dry toppings are best applied to a warm doughnut—not hot, not cold, but warm, which encourages the coating to adhere. If not enough coating sticks the first time, a second coating is perfectly acceptable.

Doughnut Troubleshooting

As with any kind of baking, it is important to use the recommended ingredients and to measure them accurately. If you make substitutions, the recipes might work, but I cannot vouch for the outcome. With doughnuts, however, there are specific areas that you should pay keen attention to:

- *Oil temperature is key.* Use a thermometer or set an accurate thermostat on your deep-fat fryer. Allow the oil to come back to the recommended temperature between batches.
- *Cut your doughnuts to the width and thickness specified,* or baking times will differ and results might suffer. I keep a ruler on hand and measure the thickness of my dough every time before I cut.
- *Always fry a test doughnut.* I give you timing and visual cues, but if your dough or batter is much colder or warmer, the frying times might be different. With doughnuts and fritters, which are sometimes as small as 1 inch across, frying 15 seconds too long can spell the difference between a dry result and a fabulous one. This is hugely important.
- *Paper towels are your friend.* When frying doughnuts, I arrange a triple layer of paper towels nearby. Use a skimmer or slotted spoon with large slots to retrieve doughnuts from the oil, allowing as much oil as possible to drain back into the pot. Place the doughnuts on the paper towels to drain. After about 10 seconds,

flip the doughnuts over onto a clean, dry area to blot the oil from the other side. I also sometimes take a clean paper towel, place it on top of the doughnuts, and give them a final pat down. The point is to gently remove as much oil as possible. Replace your paper towels frequently so that every doughnut is placed on a clean paper towel.

• *Serve and enjoy your doughnuts as soon as possible.* Doughnuts do not keep well. A doughnut that is delectable within 15 minutes of frying will change texture with every few minutes that pass; after a few hours it will have dried out. There is no way to avoid this; it is the nature of the beast. To paraphrase that doughnut maker we all grew up with, "Time to eat the doughnuts!"

The
Master Recipes

Baked Doughnuts

These doughnuts are flavored with nutmeg, but feel free to leave it out if you want a more neutral background. They lend themselves to variation: Add minced dried fruit, nuts, or even chocolate chips—see Chocolate Chip Ganache-Glazed Baked Doughnuts (page 76). The batter is loose, so you must use a doughnut pan; I use two standard-size Norpro nonstick donut pans, which hold 6 doughnuts each. These doughnuts bake up spongy and light and can be topped or glazed however you like. These are best eaten as soon as possible after baking.

Yield: *twelve 3½-inch doughnuts*

INGREDIENTS

2 cups all-purpose flour
½ cup sifted cake flour
¾ cup sugar
2 teaspoons baking powder
1 teaspoon salt
½ teaspoon baking soda
½ teaspoon freshly grated nutmeg
¼ cup (½ stick) cold unsalted butter, cut into pieces
2 large eggs, at room temperature
1 cup full-fat sour cream
2 teaspoons pure vanilla extract

Pastry bag fitted with a ½-inch round tip (such as Ateco #806)

DIRECTIONS

1. Position a rack in the middle of the oven. Preheat the oven to 350°F. Coat two standard-size doughnut pans (12 wells total) with nonstick cooking spray.

2. Whisk together both flours, the sugar, baking powder, salt, baking soda, and nutmeg in a large bowl to aerate and combine.

3. Cut the butter into the dry mixture using a pastry blender or electric mixer until combined and sandy in texture. Tiny bits of butter should be scattered evenly throughout the dry mixture.

4. Whisk the eggs in a medium-size bowl until frothy. Gently whisk in the sour cream and vanilla. Pour the wet ingredients over the dry mixture and whisk just until combined; change to a wooden spoon to combine if necessary. Scrape the mixture into the pastry bag and pipe the batter evenly among the wells of the prepared pans. Firmly tap the bottoms of the pans on the work surface to dislodge any bubbles.

5. Bake until a toothpick inserted in the center shows a few moist crumbs when removed, 10 to 12 minutes. Cool the pans on racks for about 5 minutes. Unmold the doughnuts directly onto the racks to cool completely.

6. Apply dry toppings or glaze as desired.

Baked Chocolate Doughnuts

These very dark, sweet, soft doughnuts must be formed in a doughnut pan because this batter has a pouring consistency and cannot be rolled out and cut. I use two standard-size Norpro nonstick donut pans, which hold 6 doughnuts each. These are the moistest doughnuts in the book. Some find their texture too cakey and not very doughnut-like; I say they are just at the soft cake end of the doughnut spectrum. These doughnuts will keep for 2 days in an airtight container at room temperature.

Yield: *twelve 3½-inch doughnuts*

INGREDIENTS

- 1 ½ cups all-purpose flour
- 1 cup sugar
- ¼ cup plus 1 tablespoon sifted black cocoa (see Doughnut Tip)
- ¼ cup plus 1 tablespoon sifted natural cocoa
- 1 teaspoon baking soda
- ½ teaspoon salt
- 1 cup warm water
- ⅓ cup flavorless vegetable oil, such as canola
- 1 tablespoon apple cider vinegar or distilled white vinegar
- 1 ½ teaspoons pure vanilla extract

DIRECTIONS

1. Position a rack in the middle of the oven. Preheat the oven to 350°F. Coat two standard-size doughnut pans (12 wells total) with nonstick cooking spray.

2. Whisk together the flour, sugar, both cocoas, baking soda, and salt in a large bowl to aerate and combine.

3. Whisk together the water, oil, vinegar, and vanilla in a medium-size bowl. Pour the wet ingredients over the dry mixture and whisk well until combined and very smooth. Divide the batter evenly between the wells of the prepared pans. Firmly tap the bottoms of the pans on the work surface to dislodge any bubbles.

4. Bake until a toothpick inserted in the center shows a few moist crumbs when removed, about 15 minutes. Cool the pans on racks for about 10 minutes. Unmold the doughnuts directly onto the racks to cool completely.

5. Apply dry toppings or glaze as desired.

Doughnut Tip

Using black cocoa (a specialty cocoa that you can order from King Arthur Flour; see Resources, page 173) in tandem with natural cocoa is what makes these doughnuts extra dark and chocolatey. If you prefer to make them with only natural cocoa, simply double the amount.

Old-Fashioned Buttermilk Doughnuts

These cake-style doughnuts are lightly flavored with vanilla. They have a delicate texture (thanks to the inclusion of buttermilk and cake flour) when served soon after frying time but do firm up and dry out as time goes by, so they are best eaten as soon as possible.

Yield: *about sixteen 3-inch doughnuts*

INGREDIENTS

3 cups all-purpose flour
1½ cups sifted cake flour
2 teaspoons baking powder
1 teaspoon baking soda
1½ teaspoons salt
1 cup sugar
2 large eggs, at room temperature
1 cup buttermilk, at room temperature
6 tablespoons (¾ stick) unsalted butter, melted and cooled
1 tablespoon pure vanilla extract
1 teaspoon freshly grated nutmeg
Flavorless vegetable oil for deep-frying, such as canola

DIRECTIONS

1. Whisk together both flours, the baking powder, baking soda, and salt in a large bowl to aerate and combine.

2. In another large bowl, beat together the sugar and eggs with an electric mixer until pale and creamy, or whisk well by hand. Beat in the buttermilk, butter, vanilla, and nutmeg until combined. Add the dry mixture in two batches and stir with a wooden spoon just until the dough comes together. Cover and refrigerate for at least 2 hours or up to overnight.

3. Remove the dough from the refrigerator. Line a rimmed baking sheet pan with a triple layer of paper towels. Heat 3 inches of oil in a deep pot or deep-fat fryer to 350° to 355°F.

4. While the oil is heating, dust the work surface with flour. Scrape the dough onto the surface, dust the top of the dough lightly with flour, and roll out to ½-inch thickness. Cut out doughnuts with a lightly floured 3-inch round cutter. Gently gather the scraps, press them together, roll out the dough, and cut out as many additional doughnuts as possible.

5. Fry a few doughnuts at a time; do not crowd. Fry until light golden brown, about 1 minute and 15 seconds, flip them over, and fry for about 1 minute and 15 seconds more, until light golden brown on the other side as well. Using a slotted spoon, remove each doughnut from the oil and drain thoroughly on paper towels. Repeat with the remaining doughnuts.

6. Apply dry toppings or glaze as desired.

Mashed Potato Doughnuts

This is my favorite "plain" cake-style doughnut—crisp outside, tender and rich inside, with a slightly dense, velvety crumb. Even though the flavor is neutral and works well with any glaze, do not skimp on the vanilla extract or nutmeg; they are needed for balance. These doughnuts are best eaten as soon as possible. This recipe halves well.

Yield: *about eighteen 3-inch doughnuts*

INGREDIENTS

- 3 cups all-purpose flour
- 1 cup sifted cake flour
- 1 tablespoon baking powder
- 2 teaspoons salt
- 1⅓ cups sugar
- 4 large eggs, at room temperature
- 2 cups lightly packed baked starchy baking potato, cooled (see Doughnut Tip)
- ¼ cup (½ stick) unsalted butter, melted and cooled
- ½ cup whole milk, at room temperature
- 2 teaspoons freshly grated nutmeg
- 2 teaspoons pure vanilla extract
- Flavorless vegetable oil for deep-frying, such as canola

Doughnut Tip

Use a starchy potato, such as a russet, and either bake it or microwave it on the "baked potato" setting. I use a pastry blender to mash it finely.

DIRECTIONS

1. Whisk together both flours, the baking powder, and salt in a large bowl to aerate and combine.

2. In another large bowl, beat together the sugar and eggs with an electric mixer until pale and creamy, or whisk well by hand. Beat in the potatoes, butter, milk, nutmeg, and vanilla just until combined. Add the dry mixture in two batches and stir with a wooden spoon just until the dough comes together. Cover and refrigerate for at least 2 hours or up to overnight.

3. Remove the dough from the refrigerator. Line a rimmed baking sheet pan with a triple layer of paper towels. Heat 3 inches of oil in a deep pot or deep-fat fryer to 350° to 355°F.

4. While the oil is heating, dust the work surface with flour. Scrape the dough onto the surface, dust the top of the dough lightly with flour, and roll out to ½-inch thickness. Cut out doughnuts with a lightly floured 3-inch round cutter. Gently gather the scraps, press them together, roll out the dough, and cut out as many additional doughnuts as possible.

5. Fry a few doughnuts at a time; do not crowd. Fry until light golden brown, about 1 minute and 15 seconds, flip them over, and fry for about 1 minute and 15 seconds more, until light golden brown on the other side as well. Using a slotted spoon, remove each doughnut from the oil and drain thoroughly on paper towels. Repeat with the remaining doughnuts.

6. Apply dry toppings or glaze as desired.

Sour Cream Doughnuts

These rich doughnuts have a velvety texture you can achieve only with the use of sour cream. Although they sound fancy, these are a fabulous "basic" doughnut for a wide variety of toppings and glazes. They are best enjoyed as soon as possible.

Yield: *about twelve 3-inch doughnuts*

INGREDIENTS

2½ cups all-purpose flour
1 cup sifted cake flour
1 tablespoon baking powder
½ teaspoon baking soda
1 teaspoon salt
1 cup sugar
2 large eggs, at room temperature
1 cup full-fat sour cream, at room temperature
5 tablespoons unsalted butter, melted and cooled
1½ teaspoons pure vanilla extract
½ teaspoon freshly grated nutmeg
Flavorless vegetable oil for deep-frying, such as canola

VARIATIONS

For Cardamom–Sour Cream Doughnuts, substitute 1½ teaspoons ground cardamom for the nutmeg and 1 teaspoon pure almond extract for the vanilla.

For Coconut–Sour Cream Doughnuts, substitute ½ cup unsweetened coconut milk (not cream of coconut) for ½ cup of the sour cream and fold ⅔ cup lightly packed sweetened long-shred coconut into the final batter.

DIRECTIONS

1. Whisk together both flours, the baking powder, baking soda, and salt in a large bowl to aerate and combine.

2. In another large bowl, beat together the sugar and eggs with an electric mixer until pale and creamy, or whisk well by hand. Beat in the sour cream, butter, vanilla, and nutmeg until combined. Add the dry mixture in two batches and stir with a wooden spoon just until the dough comes together. Cover and refrigerate for at least 2 hours or up to overnight.

3. Remove the dough from the refrigerator. Line a rimmed baking sheet pan with a triple layer of paper towels. Heat 3 inches of oil in a deep pot or deep-fat fryer to 350° to 355°F.

4. While the oil is heating, dust the work surface with flour. Scrape the dough onto the surface, dust the top of the dough lightly with flour, and roll out to ½-inch thickness. Cut out doughnuts with a lightly floured 3-inch round cutter. Gently gather the scraps, press them together, roll out the dough, and cut out as many additional doughnuts as possible.

5. Fry a few doughnuts at a time; do not crowd. Fry until light golden brown, about 1 minute and 15 seconds, flip them over, and fry for about 1 minute and 15 seconds more, until light golden brown on the other side as well. Using a slotted spoon, remove each doughnut from the oil and drain thoroughly on paper towels. Repeat with the remaining dough.

6. Apply dry toppings or glaze as desired.

French Crullers

A classic French choux paste (think: cream puffs) is piped into doughnut-ring shapes and then deep-fried, yielding the lightest and most elegant of doughnuts—tender yet crisp outside, light and airy inside. These are best enjoyed as soon as possible.

Yield: *about nine 3-inch crullers*

INGREDIENTS

- ½ cup plus 2 tablespoons water
- ½ cup plus 2 tablespoons whole milk
- ½ cup (1 stick) unsalted butter, at room temperature, cut into pieces
- 1 teaspoon salt
- 1 teaspoon sugar
- 1 cup all-purpose flour
- 3 large eggs, at room temperature
- Flavorless vegetable oil for deep-frying, such as canola

Pastry bag fitted with a large star decorating tip (such as Ateco #847)

DIRECTIONS

1. Cut nine 5-inch squares of parchment paper, arrange them on two rimmed baking sheet pans, and coat them thoroughly with nonstick cooking spray. Line another rimmed baking sheet pan with a triple layer of paper towels.

2. Combine the water, milk, butter, salt, and sugar in a medium-size saucepan over medium-high heat. Bring to a rolling boil; remove from the heat.

3. Quickly stir in the flour all at once until the batter comes together. Place over very low heat and stir until the dough dries out, 1 minute or less. The mixture should come away cleanly from the sides of the saucepan. Scrape the dough into the bowl of a stand mixer fitted with a paddle attachment.

4. Turn the mixer on medium and add the eggs one at a time, allowing each to be absorbed before continuing. The batter should be smooth and firm enough to hold a shape when mounded with a spoon.

5. Scrape the dough into the pastry bag. Pipe a 3-inch ring onto each parchment square. It is fine if the ends of the ring overlap a bit. If the end sticks to the pastry tip, use kitchen scissors to snip it free.

6. Heat 3 inches of oil in a deep pot or deep-fat fryer to 350° to 355°F. When the oil is hot enough, pick up one parchment square at a time and carefully but swiftly invert it so that the cruller slides into the oil (take care not to let your fingers touch the hot oil). Fry a few at a time; do not crowd. Fry until golden brown, about 2 minutes, flip them over, and fry for about 2 minutes more, until golden brown on the other side as well. Using a slotted spoon, remove each cruller from the oil and drain thoroughly on paper towels. Repeat with the remaining crullers.

7. Apply dry toppings or glaze as desired.

Chocolate Cake-Style Doughnuts

In my research and development of this book, I made dozens of chocolate doughnuts, and they were all disappointing. Either they were too light to be considered chocolatey, or they were dry as a bone. I found that including both chocolate and Dutch-processed cocoa provided the depth of color and flavor I was looking for and using oil, as opposed to butter, gave a bit of moist spring to the doughnut. These doughnuts are perfect paired with any of the glazes that follow in this section, and don't miss out on tossing them with Cinnamon-Sugar Topping (page 41), which is fabulous.

Yield: *about fourteen 3-inch doughnuts*

INGREDIENTS

2½ cups all-purpose flour
1 cup plus 2 tablespoons sifted cake flour
½ cup sifted Dutch-processed cocoa powder
1 tablespoon baking powder
1 teaspoon salt
½ teaspoon baking soda
¼ cup flavorless vegetable oil, such as canola
2 ounces semisweet chocolate (not more than 55% cacao), such as Callebaut or Ghirardelli
1 cup sugar
3 large eggs, at room temperature
1 tablespoon pure vanilla extract
1 cup buttermilk, at room temperature
Flavorless vegetable oil for deep-frying, such as canola

DIRECTIONS

1. Whisk together both flours, the cocoa, baking powder, salt, and baking soda in a large bowl to aerate and combine.

2. Heat the oil and chocolate together in a microwave or the top of a double boiler until the chocolate melts. Whisk until smooth; remove from the heat and cool slightly.

3. In another large bowl, beat together the sugar and eggs with an electric mixer until pale and creamy, or whisk well by hand. Beat in the vanilla along with the melted chocolate mixture, then add the buttermilk and beat until combined. Add the dry mixture in two batches and stir with a wooden spoon just until the dough comes together. The dough will be fairly soft. Cover and refrigerate for at least 2 hours or up to overnight.

4. Line a rimmed baking sheet pan with a triple layer of paper towels. Heat 3 inches of oil in a deep pot or deep-fat fryer to 350° to 355°F.

5. While the oil is heating, dust the work surface generously with flour. Scrape half of the dough onto the surface, dust the top of the dough lightly with flour, and roll out to ½-inch thickness. Cut out doughnuts with a lightly floured 3-inch round cutter. Gently gather the scraps, press them together, roll out the dough, and cut out as many additional doughnuts as possible. Repeat with the remaining dough.

COMBOS TO CONSIDER

Once I got into my doughnut-making zone, cranking them out every day for months, the flavor and texture combinations were literally coming to me in my sleep. I couldn't include them all in full-recipe form, but I wanted to share some possible combinations that you can put together with the recipes in this book. If you get inspired to create your own combinations, send your photos and ideas to me at dede@dedewilson.com. I can't wait to see them—and taste them!

- **Glazed Chocolate Doughnuts:** Choose any yeast-raised doughnut and cover with your choice of chocolate glaze.

- **Custard and Jelly Doughnuts:** Choose any yeast-raised doughnut and, using the filling-prior-to-frying technique (page 13), fill them with about 1½ teaspoons of your choice of jam or jelly. After frying, pipe an additional 1½ teaspoons Pastry Cream (page 42) into each doughnut.

- **Chocolate-Glazed Maple-Bacon Doughnuts:** Start with Maple-Bacon Doughnuts (page 126) and add a thick drizzle of Dark Chocolate Ganache Glaze (page 39) on top of the bacon.

- **White Chocolate–Raspberry Doughnuts:** Choose any yeast-raised doughnut and, either before or after frying, fill with about 1 tablespoon raspberry jam or jelly. Then cover each doughnut with White Chocolate Truffle Glaze (page 169) and white chocolate curls, and sprinkle with dehydrated raspberries.

- **Quadruple-Chocolate Mousse Doughnuts:** Start with Chocolate Yeast-Raised Doughnuts (page 30), filled after frying with about 1 tablespoon Chocolate Mousse (page 83). Then dip each doughnut in your choice of chocolate glaze, and top with chocolate shavings.

- **Orange-Glazed Cranberry-Filled Doughnuts:** Choose any yeast-raised doughnut and, using the filling-prior-to-frying technique (page 13), fill with about 1 tablespoon homemade or canned chunky cranberry sauce, then finish with a brushing of Citrus Glaze made with orange juice (page 35).

- **Crazy for Candy Doughnuts:** Choose any cake-style doughnut, coat with your choice of glaze, and sprinkle with your favorite crumbled candy bar. Or try a yeast-raised doughnut cut into 2½-inch rounds (no filling, though). Cover it with a chocolate glaze and your favorite crushed or chopped candy bar, such as Butterfinger or Snickers.

6. Fry a few doughnuts at a time; do not crowd. Fry for about 1 minute and 40 seconds, flip them over, and fry for about 1 minute and 40 seconds more on the other side, until just cooked through. (See Doughnut Tip.) Using a slotted spoon, remove each doughnut from the oil and drain thoroughly on paper towels. Repeat with the remaining doughnuts.

7. Apply dry toppings or glaze as desired.

Doughnut Tip

Chocolate doughnuts are so dark that it is hard to tell when they are done; frying and testing a sample doughnut is a must.

Basic Yeast-Raised Doughnuts

These doughnuts are yeast raised, spongy, and light, yet with a bit of substance to their texture. The flavor is fairly neutral, which allows them to match well with custards, jelly, and all sorts of fillings and glazes. Turn to this recipe for classic Jelly Doughnuts (page 124) or Boston Cream Doughnuts (page 58). These are best enjoyed as soon as possible.

Yield: *about twenty-eight 2½-inch round doughnuts or about twenty-four 3-inch ring-shaped doughnuts*

INGREDIENTS

⅔ cup warm water (110° to 115°F)

Two 0.25-ounce packages active dry yeast

¼ cup (½ stick) unsalted butter, at room temperature, cut into pieces

⅔ cup whole milk

⅔ cup sugar

2 large eggs, at room temperature, beaten

1½ teaspoons salt

1 teaspoon freshly grated nutmeg

1 teaspoon pure vanilla extract

5 to 5¼ cups all-purpose flour

Flavorless vegetable oil for deep-frying, such as canola

DIRECTIONS

1. Place the warm water in a large bowl and sprinkle the yeast over it. Stir to combine and let sit for 5 minutes.

2. Meanwhile, melt the butter with the milk in a microwave or in a saucepan on the stovetop, then cool to lukewarm (110° to 115°F). Add the milk mixture, sugar, eggs, salt, nutmeg, vanilla, and 2½ cups of the flour to the yeast and stir with a wooden spoon or silicone spatula until combined and smooth. The mixture will have some body but will still be very wet and loose. Add another 2½ cups of the flour and stir until the mixture becomes a very slightly sticky, elastic dough, adding more of the remaining ¼ cup flour only if necessary. Knead well by beating vigorously with the spoon or spatula, or use the flat paddle or dough hook of a stand mixer. The mixture should be elastic, yet slightly sticky and not dry.

3. Scrape the dough into a buttered bowl, making sure there is plenty of headroom. Cover the bowl with plastic wrap and place in a warm, draft-free location to rise until doubled in size, about 1 hour.

4. Generously flour two rimmed baking sheet pans. Gently punch down the dough and divide it in half. Roll out one piece of dough on a lightly floured work surface to ½-inch thickness. Cut out doughnuts with a lightly floured cutter. Use a 2½-inch round cutter for filled doughnuts or a 3-inch ring-shaped doughnut cutter for a classic doughnut shape. Repeat with the remaining dough. Gently

gather the scraps, press them together, roll out the dough, and cut out as many additional doughnuts as possible. Place the doughnuts, well spaced, on the prepared pans. Let rise in a warm, draft-free location until doubled in size, about 30 minutes.

5. Line two rimmed baking sheet pans with a triple layer of paper towels. Heat 3 inches of oil in a deep pot or deep-fat fryer to 350° to 355°F. When the oil is hot enough, fry a few doughnuts at a time; do not crowd. Fry until light golden brown, about 1½ minutes, flip them over, and fry for about 1½ minutes more, until light golden brown on the other side as well. Using a slotted spoon, remove each doughnut from the oil and drain thoroughly on paper towels. Repeat with the remaining doughnuts.

6. Apply dry toppings, fill, or glaze as desired.

Doughnut Tips

Researching this style of doughnut was quite an education. Many recipes yielded doughnuts so light that they practically disappeared in my mouth before I could taste them, while those made with bread flour were tough. Most were flavorless. The amounts of salt, vanilla, and nutmeg in this dough give it enough flavor, but not so much so that any one ingredient becomes obvious or dominant. Note that I suggest making these doughnuts 2½ inches across if you intend to fill them. I find that larger doughnuts, if filled, become unwieldy.

Chocolate Yeast-Raised Doughnuts

Dutch-processed cocoa gives this yeast-raised doughnut a rich chocolate color and flavor. These are best enjoyed as soon as possible.

Yield: *about twenty-four 2½-inch round doughnuts or about twenty-one 3-inch ring-shaped doughnuts*

INGREDIENTS

- 4 to 4½ cups all-purpose flour
- ½ cup sifted Dutch-processed cocoa powder
- ½ cup warm water (110° to 115°F)
- Two 0.25-ounce packages active dry yeast
- 6 tablespoons (¾ stick) unsalted butter, at room temperature, cut into pieces
- ¼ cup whole milk
- ⅔ cup sugar
- 4 large eggs, at room temperature, beaten
- 2 large egg yolks, at room temperature, beaten
- 2 teaspoons salt
- 2 teaspoons pure vanilla extract
- Flavorless vegetable oil for deep-frying, such as canola

DIRECTIONS

1. Whisk together 4 cups of the flour and the cocoa in a large bowl to aerate and combine. Place the warm water in another large bowl and sprinkle the yeast over it. Stir to combine and let sit for 5 minutes.

2. Meanwhile, melt the butter with the milk in a microwave or in a saucepan on the stovetop, then cool to lukewarm (110° to 115°F). Add the milk mixture, sugar, whole eggs, egg yolks, salt, vanilla, and half of the flour mixture to the yeast and stir with a wooden spoon or silicone spatula until combined and smooth. The mixture will have some body but will still be very wet and loose. Stir in the remaining flour mixture until the dough becomes a very slightly sticky, elastic dough, adding the remaining ½ cup flour only if necessary. Knead well by beating vigorously with the spoon or spatula, or use the flat paddle or dough hook of a stand mixer. The mixture should be elastic, yet slightly sticky and not dry.

3. Scrape the dough into a buttered bowl, making sure there is plenty of headroom. Cover the bowl with plastic wrap and place in a warm, draft-free location to rise until doubled in size, about 1 hour 15 minutes.

4. Generously flour two rimmed baking sheet pans. Gently punch down the dough and divide it in half. Roll out one piece of dough on a lightly floured work surface to ½-inch thickness. Cut out doughnuts with a lightly floured cutter. Use a 2½-inch round cutter for filled doughnuts or a 3-inch ring-shaped doughnut cutter for a classic doughnut shape. Repeat with the remaining dough. Gently

gather the scraps, press them together, roll out the dough, and cut out as many additional doughnuts as possible. Place the doughnuts, well spaced, on the prepared pans. Let rise in a warm, draft-free location until doubled in size, about 45 minutes.

5. Line two rimmed baking sheet pans with a triple layer of paper towels. Heat 3 inches of oil in a deep pot or deep-fat fryer to 350° to 355°F. When the oil is hot enough, fry a few doughnuts at a time; do not crowd. Fry for about 1½ minutes, flip them over, and fry for about 1½ minutes more on the other side, until just cooked through. Using a slotted spoon, remove each doughnut from the oil and drain thoroughly on paper towels. Repeat with the remaining doughnuts.

6. Apply dry toppings or glaze, or fill as desired.

Doughnut Tip

These doughnuts tend to take longer to rise than those made without cocoa. Make sure that all of the ingredients are at the temperature called for—including the water.

Krispy Kreme Kopykat Doughnuts

This very famous doughnut company is known for its glazed raised doughnut, which is light, spongy, sweet, sticky, and fabulous. This is my version, based on an Internet recipe that is allegedly the real thing. I make no claims about its authenticity, but this recipe does make a very similar doughnut. The shortening yields a texture similar to that of store-bought doughnuts. This is my go-to recipe for a plain raised doughnut, as it offers the soft texture we usually expect. These doughnuts are best enjoyed as soon as possible, though they will still be soft and springy the next day.

Yield: *about twenty-six 2½-inch round doughnuts or about twenty-two 3-inch ring-shaped doughnuts*

INGREDIENTS

¼ cup warm water (110° to 115°F)

Two 0.25-ounce packages active dry yeast

6 tablespoons vegetable shortening, such as Crisco

1½ cups whole milk

½ cup sugar

2 large eggs, at room temperature, beaten

1 teaspoon salt

1 teaspoon freshly grated nutmeg

1 teaspoon pure vanilla extract

5 to 5½ cups all-purpose flour

Flavorless vegetable oil for deep-frying, such as canola

DIRECTIONS

1. Place the warm water in a large bowl and sprinkle the yeast over it. Stir to combine and let sit for 5 minutes.

2. Meanwhile, melt the shortening with the milk in a microwave or in a saucepan on the stovetop, then cool to lukewarm (110° to 115°F). Add the milk mixture, sugar, eggs, salt, nutmeg, vanilla, and 2½ cups of the flour to the yeast and stir with a wooden spoon or silicone spatula until combined and smooth. The mixture will have some body but will still be very wet and loose. Stir in another 2½ cups of the flour until the mixture becomes a very slightly sticky, elastic dough, adding more of the remaining ½ cup flour only if necessary. Knead well by beating vigorously with the spoon or spatula, or use the flat paddle or dough hook of a stand mixer.

3. Scrape the dough into a buttered bowl, making sure there is plenty of headroom. Cover the bowl with plastic wrap and place in a warm, draft-free location to rise until doubled in size, about 1 hour.

4. Generously flour two rimmed baking sheet pans. Gently punch down the dough and divide it in half. Roll out one piece of dough on a lightly floured work surface to ½-inch thickness. Cut out doughnuts with a lightly floured cutter. Use a 2½-inch round cutter for filled doughnuts or a 3-inch ring-shaped doughnut cutter for a classic doughnut

MORE COMBOS TO CONSIDER

- **Cherry-Cheese Danish Doughnuts:** Choose any yeast-raised doughnut and, using the filling-prior-to-frying technique (page 13), fill with about 1½ teaspoons canned cherry pie filling. After frying, pipe an additional 1½ teaspoons Cheesecake Filling (page 75) into each doughnut. Coat with confectioners' or superfine sugar or a simple vanilla or sugar glaze.

- **Apricot-Cheese Danish Doughnuts:** Choose any yeast-raised doughnut and, using the filling-prior-to-frying technique (page 13), fill with about 1½ teaspoons apricot preserves. After frying, pipe an additional 1½ teaspoons Cheesecake Filling (page 75) into each doughnut. Coat with confectioners' or superfine sugar or a simple vanilla or sugar glaze.

- **Orange Marmalade Doughnuts:** Choose any yeast-raised doughnut and, using the filling-prior-to-frying technique (page 13), fill with about 1 tablespoon orange marmalade. Top with Citrus Glaze made with orange juice (page 35).

- **Chocolate-Glazed Peanut Butter Doughnuts:** Start with Chocolate Yeast-Raised Doughnuts (page 30) and, using the filling-prior-to-frying technique (page 13), fill with about 1 tablespoon peanut butter (smooth or chunky). Top with your choice of chocolate glaze.

- **Caramel Apple Fritters:** Use Apple Fritters (page 44), dunked in or drizzled with Caramel Glaze (page 85).

- **Guava-Coconut Doughnuts:** Choose any yeast-raised doughnut and, using the filling-prior-to-frying technique (page 13), fill with about 1 tablespoon guava paste. Top with Coconut Glaze (page 95) and sweetened long-shred coconut.

- **Blueberry Pancake Fritters:** Use Blueberry–Sour Cream Fritters (page 56) dunked in Maple Glaze (page 171).

- **Apple Pie Doughnuts:** Start with Cider Doughnuts (page 90) and, using the filling-prior-to-frying technique (page 13), fill with about 1 tablespoon apple-pie filling. Toss with Cinnamon-Sugar Topping (page 41).

shape. Repeat with the remaining dough. Gently gather the scraps, press them together, roll out the dough, and cut out as many additional doughnuts as possible. Place the doughnuts, well spaced, on the prepared pans. Let rise in a warm, draft-free location until doubled in size, about 30 minutes.

5. Line two rimmed baking sheet pans with a triple layer of paper towels. Heat 3 inches of oil in a deep pot or deep-fat fryer to 350° to 355°F. When the oil is hot enough, fry a few doughnuts at a time; do not crowd. Fry until light golden brown, about 1½ minutes, flip them over, and fry for about 1½ minutes more, until light golden brown on the other side as well. Using a slotted spoon, remove each doughnut from the oil and drain thoroughly on paper towels. Repeat with the remaining doughnuts.

6. Apply dry toppings or glaze, or fill as desired.

Hard Sugar Glaze

This classic confectioners' sugar glaze hardens to an opaque white color as it sets. It will crackle underneath your teeth as you bite through it. Use it to dip the entire tops of your doughnuts, or drizzle it out of a parchment paper cone or with a fork or spoon. You can halve or double the recipe.

Yield: *enough to coat the tops of about twelve 3-inch doughnuts*

INGREDIENTS

2 cups sifted confectioners'
    sugar
2 tablespoons water

DIRECTIONS

Place the confectioners' sugar in a medium-size sauce-pan. Whisk in the water until it begins to combine; it will be thick before you heat it. Cook over medium heat, whisking often, until it liquefies and becomes completely smooth and very warm—but not hot—to the touch. Do not let it simmer. The cooking will be brief—about 15 seconds. Remove from the heat and use immediately.

VARIATIONS

For Hard Vanilla Glaze, whisk in ¼ teaspoon pure vanilla extract after removing the glaze from the heat.

For Hard Almond Glaze, whisk in ¼ teaspoon pure almond extract after removing the glaze from the heat.

For Hard Espresso Glaze, whisk 1 teaspoon to 1 tablespoon instant espresso powder (depending on the strength desired) into the confectioners' sugar before adding the water.

Doughnut Tip

Heating the glaze mixture leaves it ultrasmooth and is also necessary for the glaze to truly harden. The mixture will appear to be unusually dry until you begin the heating and whisking process, which cause the confectioners' sugar and water to come together.

Soft and Sheer Sugar Glaze

This confectioners' sugar glaze remains soft, sheer, and somewhat sticky. Use it to dip the entire tops of your doughnuts, or apply with a silicone pastry brush. You can halve or double the recipe.

Yield: *enough to coat the tops of about twelve 3-inch doughnuts*

INGREDIENTS

2 cups sifted confectioners' sugar

3 to 4 tablespoons water

DIRECTIONS

Place the confectioners' sugar in a medium-size bowl. Whisk in the water a little bit at a time, until the desired consistency is reached. Use immediately.

VARIATIONS

For Soft and Sheer Vanilla Glaze, whisk in ¼ teaspoon pure vanilla extract at the end of the recipe.

For Soft and Sheer Almond Glaze, whisk in ¼ teaspoon pure almond extract at the end of the recipe.

> **Doughnut Tip**
>
> Sifting the confectioners' sugar will ensure that your glaze is ultrasmooth.

Citrus Glaze

This confectioners' sugar glaze has a sharp citrus edge and remains semi-opaque and somewhat sticky when set. Use it to dip the entire tops of your doughnuts, or apply with a silicone pastry brush. You can halve or double the recipe.

Yield: *enough to coat the tops of about twelve 3-inch doughnuts*

INGREDIENTS

2 cups sifted confectioners' sugar

3 to 4 tablespoons freshly squeezed lemon juice, lime juice, or orange juice

DIRECTIONS

Place the confectioners' sugar in a medium-size bowl. Whisk in the citrus juice a little at a time until the desired consistency is achieved. Use immediately.

Spiced Orange Glaze

This confectioners' sugar–based glaze has a bright citrus flavor, accented with cinnamon and ginger. Use it to dip the entire tops of your doughnuts, or drizzle it out of a parchment paper cone or with a fork or spoon. It's perfect paired with Pumpkin Spice Doughnuts (page 140), Mashed Potato Doughnuts (page 23), or anywhere you would appreciate this flavor combo. You can halve or double the recipe.

Yield: *enough to coat the tops of about twelve 3-inch doughnuts*

INGREDIENTS

- 2 cups sifted confectioners' sugar
- 1 teaspoon ground cinnamon
- ½ teaspoon ground ginger
- 2 tablespoons freshly squeezed orange juice, or more as needed

DIRECTIONS

Place the confectioners' sugar and spices in a medium-size saucepan. Whisk in the orange juice until it begins to combine; it will be thick before you heat it. Cook over medium heat, stirring constantly, until it liquefies and becomes completely smooth and very warm—but not hot—to the touch. Do not let it simmer. The cooking will be brief—about 15 seconds. Remove from the heat and use immediately.

Doughnut Tip

Heating the mixture leaves it ultrasmooth and is also necessary for the glaze to truly harden. If you would like a soft glaze, simply whisk off the heat, in which case you will need more orange juice. Simply add more, a teaspoon at a time, until you reach the desired consistency.

Cocoa Glaze

This chocolatey glaze hardens as it sets. Use it to dip the entire tops of your doughnuts, or drizzle it out of a parchment paper cone or with a fork or spoon. You can halve or double the recipe.

Yield: *enough to coat the tops of about fifteen 3-inch doughnuts*

INGREDIENTS

- 3 cups sifted confectioners' sugar
- ½ cup sifted natural or Dutch-processed cocoa powder
- 6 tablespoons water, or more as needed

DIRECTIONS

Place the confectioners' sugar and cocoa in a medium-size saucepan. Whisk in the water until it begins to combine; it will be thick before you heat it. Cook over medium heat, whisking constantly, until it liquefies and becomes completely smooth and very warm—but not hot—to the touch. Do not let it simmer. The cooking will be brief—about 15 seconds. Remove from the heat and use immediately.

Doughnut Tip

This is a "chocolate" glaze that you can make when you have no chocolate in the house, as it uses unsweetened cocoa. Heating the mixture leaves it ultrasmooth and is also necessary for the glaze to truly harden upon cooling. If you want to save time and are willing to have a glaze that only partially hardens, you can combine the sugar and cocoa with very hot tap water. Natural cocoa will give you a cocoa-colored glaze with a lighter chocolate flavor; Dutch-processed cocoa will give you a very dark, almost black glaze with a deeper, richer flavor. Your choice.

Dark Chocolate Glaze

This chocolate glaze, based on unsweetened chocolate, becomes firm on the surface but remains a bit soft underneath as it sets. It is the middle child of the three chocolate glazes in the book—richer than Cocoa Glaze but not as decadent as Dark Chocolate Ganache Glaze. Use it to dip the entire tops of your doughnuts, or drizzle it out of a parchment paper cone or with a fork or spoon. You can halve or double the recipe.

Yield: *enough to coat the tops of about twelve 3-inch doughnuts*

INGREDIENTS

3 ounces unsweetened
  chocolate, finely chopped
¼ cup heavy cream
2 tablespoons water
2 cups sifted confectioners'
  sugar

DIRECTIONS

1. Place the chocolate, cream, and water in a medium-size saucepan and cook over low heat, stirring occasionally, until the chocolate is melted and the mixture is thick but smooth.

2. Whisk in the confectioners' sugar and cook over medium-low heat, stirring constantly, until the mixture is completely smooth and very warm—but not hot—to the touch. Do not let it simmer. The cooking will be brief—30 seconds to 1 minute. Remove from the heat and use immediately.

VARIATION

For Mocha Glaze, add 1 tablespoon instant espresso powder along with the chocolate, cream, and water.

Dark Chocolate Ganache Glaze

This chocolate glaze is essentially the same recipe as that used for truffle centers—chocolate, cream, and a bit of butter for extra richness and shine. It is the richest of the chocolate glazes in the book, so use it when you want a luxurious topping. Dip the entire tops of your doughnuts in it, or drizzle it out of a parchment paper cone or with a fork or spoon. You can halve or double the recipe. This glaze may be refrigerated in an airtight container for up to 1 week or frozen for up to 1 month. Reheat to dipping consistency before using.

Yield: *enough to coat the tops of about twenty 3-inch doughnuts*

INGREDIENTS

1 cup heavy cream
10 ounces semisweet or bittersweet chocolate (50% to 64% cacao), such as Valrhona Equatoriale, Callebaut, or Ghirardelli, finely chopped
1 tablespoon unsalted butter

DIRECTIONS

1. Place the cream in a wide 2-quart saucepan and bring to a simmer over medium heat.

2. Remove from the heat and immediately sprinkle the chocolate into the cream. Cover and let sit for 5 minutes. The heat of the cream should melt the chocolate. Gently stir the ganache until smooth. If the chocolate has not melted completely, place over very low heat and stir often until melted, taking care not to burn it.

3. Allow the glaze to cool until warm, but not hot, and still fluid. (You may hasten the chilling process by stirring over an ice bath. If it becomes too firm, or if you would like to return it to a softer state, simply place over hot water or microwave briefly.)

Peanut Butter Glaze

The Doughnut Plant in New York City is famous for many of their doughnuts, and the peanut butter and jelly doughnut is one of their most popular. This is my take on their glaze. Use it for Peanut Butter–Glazed Jelly Doughnuts (page 136), Marshmallow Fluff and Peanut Butter Doughnuts (page 128), or anytime you want that nutty flavor and texture. The combination of whole milk and smooth peanut butter will result in a smooth, rich texture.

Yield: *enough to coat the tops of about twenty-four 3-inch doughnuts*

INGREDIENTS

4½ cups sifted confectioners' sugar

1 cup smooth peanut butter (such as Skippy; do not use natural)

⅔ to 1 cup whole milk

½ cup chopped peanuts (unsalted or lightly salted)

DIRECTIONS

1. Place the confectioners' sugar in a large bowl.

2. In a small saucepan, heat the peanut butter with ⅔ cup of the milk over medium-low heat until the mixture is hot but not simmering. Remove from the heat and gently whisk the peanut butter into the milk so that it begins to soften—it will not dissolve into the milk, which is okay.

3. Scrape the milk and peanut butter over the confectioners' sugar and whisk vigorously until smooth. Add the additional ⅓ cup milk only if needed to make a smooth, pourable glaze. Stir in the peanuts. You can dip the tops of your doughnuts right in the glaze or spread it on top of the doughnuts using a small offset spatula. (If the glaze drips off the doughnuts too readily, simply cool it a little before dipping.) Let the glazed doughnuts sit until the glaze sets, about 5 minutes. Serve immediately.

Cinnamon-Sugar Topping

This simple combination of cinnamon and sugar is a classic dry topping for doughnuts. Try it with Cider Doughnuts (page 90), Blueberry–Sour Cream Fritters (page 56), and Chocolate Cake-Style Doughnuts (page 26) in particular. You can halve or double the recipe. It will keep for 1 week in an airtight container at room temperature.

Yield: *enough to coat the tops of about sixteen 3-inch doughnuts or about 24 doughnut holes or small fritters*

INGREDIENTS

1 cup granulated sugar or superfine sugar
1½ teaspoons ground cinnamon

DIRECTIONS

Stir the sugar and cinnamon together in a shallow bowl large enough to hold a doughnut. Place a still-warm doughnut on top of the mixture and toss around to coat thoroughly.

Doughnut Tip

If you want a finely textured topping, use superfine sugar. My version of this topping is moderately flavored with cinnamon. Feel free to scale up or down on the spice if you like.

Cream Cheese Frosting

This classic cream cheese frosting is formulated to be the right sweetness to complement most doughnuts and is also creamy enough to spread easily. You can halve or double the recipe. Use immediately for best results or store for up to 3 days in an airtight container in the refrigerator; bring to room temperature and rebeat before using.

Yield: *enough to coat the tops of about eighteen 2½-inch doughnuts*

INGREDIENTS

2 cups sifted confectioners' sugar
One 8-ounce package cream cheese, at room temperature, cut into pieces
½ cup (1 stick) unsalted butter, at room temperature, cut into pieces
1 teaspoon pure vanilla extract

DIRECTIONS

Place all of the ingredients in a medium-size bowl and beat with an electric mixer until it begins to combine. Scrape the bowl down once or twice and keep beating until satiny smooth and creamy.

Doughnut Tip

I like to use full-fat cream cheese, but you could substitute Neufchâtel cheese, although the texture of the frosting will be a bit softer. Bring your cheese to room temperature before beating and the frosting will come together effortlessly.

Pastry Cream

This sweet and smooth vanilla-flavored pastry cream, thickened with cornstarch, is featured in Boston Cream Doughnuts (page 58), and a variation is used in Vanilla Bean Custard Doughnuts (page 164). It will keep for up to 2 days in an airtight container in the refrigerator. The recipe does make a generous amount, and you can halve it, but I find it easier to prepare this amount and use the extra for other desserts.

Yield: *about 2½ cups, enough to fill about 40 doughnuts*

INGREDIENTS

2 cups whole milk
2 large eggs, at room temperature
2 large egg yolks, at room temperature
½ cup plus 2 tablespoons sugar
2 tablespoons cornstarch
Pinch of salt
2 tablespoons unsalted butter, at room temperature, cut into pieces
1 teaspoon pure vanilla extract

Doughnut Tips

If there are lumps in your pastry cream when you remove it from the heat, simply press it through a fine mesh strainer (pastry chefs do this all the time!). If you would like it a tad less sweet, use ½ cup sugar. Make sure to use whole milk for the creamiest consistency.

DIRECTIONS

1. Bring the milk to a boil in a medium-size nonreactive saucepan over medium heat; remove from the heat and cover to keep warm.

2. Whisk together the whole eggs, egg yolks, and sugar in a medium-size bowl until creamy. Whisk in the cornstarch and salt until smooth.

3. Pour about one quarter of the warm milk over the egg mixture, whisking gently. Add the remaining milk and whisk to combine. Immediately pour the mixture back into the pot and cook over medium to heat. Whisk almost continuously and watch for bubbles. As soon as the mixture comes to a boil, whisk vigorously and constantly for 1 to 2 minutes. The pastry cream is ready when it is thick enough to mound when dropped from a spoon but still satiny.

4. Remove from the heat and whisk in the butter and vanilla. Allow the pastry cream to cool; stir occasionally to release the heat. When almost at room temperature, scrape into an airtight container, press plastic wrap directly against the surface (to keep a skin from forming), cover, and refrigerate for at least 4 hours or until thoroughly chilled before using.

VARIATION

For Rich Vanilla Pastry Cream, slit 1 plump, moist vanilla bean lengthwise and scrape all of the tiny seeds into the milk in step 1. This is most easily accomplished with the tip of a teaspoon or butter knife. Add the outer bean pieces as well. Bring the milk just to a boil over medium heat; remove from the heat, cover, and steep for 15 minutes. Remove the outer bean pieces and rewarm the milk. Proceed with the recipe as directed above.

The
Field Guide

Apple Fritters

DESCRIPTION *These are very rustic-looking fritters made with whole milk, tart and sweet apples, a bit of cinnamon, and lemon zest. Finish them off with a roll in Cinnamon-Sugar Topping or Cider Syrup Glaze, or do half a batch in each.*

FIELD NOTES *The combination of tart and sweet apples creates a nice balance in this fried treat. Granny Smith is a must for the tart apple; the sweet apple could be Cortland, McIntosh, Empire, Ida Red, or even Golden Delicious. The fritters must be somewhat flat when they go in the oil—if they are spherical, they will not cook through. Cider syrup is a specialty product that you might have to order from King Arthur Flour (see Resources, page 173). It is apple cider boiled down to a syrupy consistency. The glaze made with this is concentrated with apple flavor.*

LIFESPAN *These are best eaten as soon as possible.*

Yield: *about ten 3-inch fritters*

INGREDIENTS

Doughnuts:
2 cups all-purpose flour
3 tablespoons firmly packed dark brown sugar
1 tablespoon baking powder
1 teaspoon ground cinnamon
1 teaspoon salt
2 large eggs, at room temperature
⅔ cup whole milk
1½ tablespoons unsalted butter, melted
1½ tablespoons flavorless vegetable oil, such as canola, plus more for deep-frying

1 teaspoon finely grated lemon zest
2½ cups 1-inch chunks peeled and cored apples (from 1 large tart apple and 1 large sweet apple; see Field Notes)

Cider syrup glaze:
5 tablespoons cider syrup (see Field Notes)
1½ cups sifted confectioners' sugar
¾ teaspoon ground cinnamon

Half a recipe Cinnamon-Sugar Topping (page 41)

DIRECTIONS

1. Whisk together the flour, brown sugar, baking powder, cinnamon, and salt in a small bowl to aerate and combine.

2. Whisk together the eggs, milk, melted butter, 1½ tablespoons oil, and lemon zest in a large bowl. Fold in the dry mixture until a few streaks of flour remain. Gently fold in the apples until just combined.

3. Line a rimmed baking sheet pan with a triple layer of paper towels. Heat 3 inches of oil in a deep pot or deep-fat fryer to 350° to 355°F. When the oil is hot enough, use two large spoons to scoop up an amount of batter about the size of a tennis ball. Use one spoon to flatten the mound of batter, so that you drop a thick disk of batter, not a ball, into the oil. Fry a few at a time; do not crowd. Fry until golden brown,

about 1 minute and 40 seconds, flip them over, and fry for about 1 minute and 40 seconds more, until golden brown on the other side as well. Using a slotted spoon, remove each fritter from the oil and drain thoroughly on paper towels. Repeat with the remaining batter.

4. *For the glaze*: In a medium-size saucepan set over low heat, heat the cider syrup just until warm. Whisk in the confectioners' sugar and cinnamon until completely smooth. Using a teaspoon, drizzle the glaze over half of the batch of fritters (still resting on paper towels) while they are still warm; let sit for about 5 minutes to allow the glaze to set. Roll the other half of the batch in the cinnamon-sugar topping, coating all sides.

Apricot-Cardamom Doughnuts

 **DESCRIPTION** *This is a not-too-sweet, somewhat sophisticated doughnut. The apricot and cardamom flavors are subtle, but present, and take the form of minced dried apricots and ground spice. The apricot flavor is further bolstered by an apricot icing made with apricot nectar and confectioners' sugar.*

 **FIELD NOTES** *Cardamom is a bold spice that can easily take over the flavor of a dish. Frying seems to mute flavors, though, so the large amount of cardamom in this recipe is correct. For the glaze, you can use apricot nectar, which usually contains added sugar and is easy to find; however, if you search a little harder, perhaps at Whole Foods Market or a similar store, you can find an apricot juice that is 100 percent juice, which will give you more apricot flavor.*

 **LIFESPAN** *These are best eaten as soon as possible.*

Yield: *about twelve 3-inch doughnuts*

INGREDIENTS

Apricot glaze:
2 cups sifted confectioners' sugar
3 to 4 tablespoons apricot nectar

1 recipe Cardamom–Sour Cream
Doughnuts (page 24), prepared with
1 cup finely minced dried apricots folded
into the final dough, cut into 3-inch rings,
fried, and beginning to cool

DIRECTIONS

1. Place the confectioners' sugar in a medium-size bowl. Whisk in the apricot nectar a little bit at a time until the desired consistency is reached.

2. While the doughnuts are still slightly warm, dip the tops in the glaze and let sit for about 5 minutes to allow the glaze to set.

Banana Doughnuts with Banana Glaze

DESCRIPTION *Like your favorite banana bread, this doughnut is moist with mashed ripe banana. The glaze has banana in it too, further boosting the flavor.*

FIELD NOTES *Make sure your bananas are completely ripe—they should be soft and have a potent banana aroma, and the skin should have no green (and preferably some black spots). These bananas will yield the best flavor. The amount of lemon juice in the glaze is enough to keep the glaze from discoloring.*

LIFESPAN *These are best eaten as soon as possible.*

Yield: *about ten 3-inch doughnuts*

INGREDIENTS

Doughnuts:
2 cups all-purpose flour
½ cup sifted cake flour
2½ teaspoons baking powder
½ teaspoon baking soda
½ teaspoon salt
¼ teaspoon freshly grated nutmeg
½ cup firmly packed light brown sugar
2 large eggs, at room temperature
½ cup lightly mashed very ripe banana

½ cup full-fat sour cream, at room
 temperature
1 teaspoon pure vanilla extract
Flavorless vegetable oil for deep-frying,
 such as canola

Banana glaze:
½ cup lightly mashed very ripe banana
2 teaspoons freshly squeezed lemon juice
1 cup sifted confectioners' sugar

DIRECTIONS

1. *For the doughnuts*: Whisk together both flours, the baking powder, baking soda, salt, and nutmeg in a medium-size bowl to aerate and combine.

2. Beat the brown sugar and eggs together in a large bowl with an electric mixer until pale and creamy, or whisk well by hand. Beat in the mashed banana, sour cream, and vanilla just until combined. Add the dry mixture in two batches and stir with a wooden spoon just until the dough comes together. Cover and refrigerate for at least 2 hours or up to overnight.

3. Remove the dough from the refrigerator. Line a rimmed baking sheet pan with a triple layer of paper towels. Heat 3 inches of oil in a deep pot or deep-fat fryer to 350° to 355°F.

4. While the oil is heating, dust the work surface generously with flour. Scrape the dough onto the surface (it will be very soft), dust the top of the dough lightly with flour, and roll out to ½-inch thickness. Cut out doughnuts

with a lightly floured 3-inch round cutter. Gently gather the scraps, press them together, roll out the dough, and cut out as many additional doughnuts as possible.

5. Fry a few doughnuts at a time; do not crowd. Fry until light golden brown, about 1½ minutes, flip them over, and fry for about 1½ minutes more, until light golden brown on the other side as well. Using a slotted spoon, remove each doughnut from the oil and drain thoroughly on paper towels. Repeat with the remaining doughnuts.

6. *For the glaze*: Whisk together the mashed banana and lemon juice in a medium-size bowl until combined; there will still be some small bits of banana. Whisk in the confectioners' sugar until the glaze is combined and fluid.

7. While the doughnuts are still slightly warm, dip the tops in the glaze and let sit for about 5 minutes to allow the glaze to set.

Basic Baked Doughnuts with Cinnamon Sugar

 **DESCRIPTION** *The tops of baked doughnuts are dipped in melted butter and then cinnamon sugar.*

 **FIELD NOTES** *These are considerably lighter than any of the fried versions. If you are looking for a basic baked doughnut, this is the perfect recipe. I like to dip just the tops in butter and cinnamon sugar to keep them on the lighter side, but feel free to dunk and roll them in their entirety for a richer version. If you do so, you'll need to double the amount of butter and cinnamon sugar.*

 **LIFESPAN** *These are best eaten the day they are made.*

Yield: *twelve 3½-inch doughnuts*

INGREDIENTS

5 tablespoons unsalted butter
Half a recipe Cinnamon-Sugar Topping
(page 41)

1 recipe Baked Doughnuts (page 20),
baked and beginning to cool

DIRECTIONS

1. Melt the butter in a shallow bowl in the microwave. Place the cinnamon-sugar topping in another shallow bowl.

2. While the doughnuts are still slightly warm, dip the tops first in the melted butter and then in the cinnamon sugar.

Beignets

🔸 **DESCRIPTION** *These rectangular yeast-risen pastries are topped with a generous shower of confectioners' sugar.*

🔸 **FIELD NOTES** *If you look up recipes for beignets, you will find that some are based on pâte à choux, like my French Crullers (page 25), while others are yeast-based, such as these. If you visit New Orleans, you will find yeasty, pillowy beignets everywhere; locals enjoy them for breakfast with chicory-laced coffee. The dough itself is not very sweet, which goes wonderfully with the copious amounts of confectioners' sugar that you will sprinkle on top. For a double dose, roll them in confectioners' sugar first, then sprinkle extra on top using a strainer or sugar-shaker.*

🔸 **LIFESPAN** *These are best eaten as soon as possible.*

C

Yield: *about 20 beignets*

INGREDIENTS

⅔ cup warm water (110° to 115°F)
One 0.25-ounce package active dry yeast
3 tablespoons vegetable shortening
½ cup whole milk
¼ cup granulated sugar
1 large egg, at room temperature, beaten

½ teaspoon salt
3½ to 3¾ cups all-purpose flour
Flavorless vegetable oil for deep-frying,
 such as canola
Confectioners' sugar

DIRECTIONS

1. Place the warm water in a large bowl and sprinkle the yeast over it. Stir to combine and let sit for 5 minutes.

2. Melt the shortening with the milk in a microwave or a small saucepan on the stovetop, then cool to lukewarm (110° to 115°F). Add the shortening mixture, granulated sugar, egg, salt, and 2½ cups of the flour to the yeast mixture and stir with a wooden spoon or silicone spatula until combined and smooth. The mixture will have some body but will still be very wet and loose. Stir in another 1 cup of the flour until the mixture becomes a slightly sticky, elastic dough, adding the remaining ¼ cup flour only if necessary. Knead well by beating vigorously with the spoon or spatula or use the flat paddle or dough hook of a stand mixer. The mixture should be elastic, yet slightly sticky and not dry.

3. Scrape the dough into a buttered bowl, making sure there is plenty of headroom. Cover the bowl with plastic wrap and place in warm, draft-free location to rise until doubled in size, about 1 hour.

4. Generously flour two rimmed baking sheet pans. Gently punch down the dough. On a lightly floured work surface, roll out a large rectangle of dough ½ inch thick. Cut the dough with a pizza wheel into 3 x 2-inch rectangles. Place the rectangles, well spaced, on the prepared pans. Let rise in a warm, draft-free location until doubled in size, about 30 minutes.

5. Line two rimmed baking sheet pans with a triple layer of paper towels. Heat 3 inches of oil in a deep pot or deep-fat fryer to 350° to 355°F. When the oil is hot enough, fry a few beignets at a time; do not crowd. Fry until light golden brown, about 1 minute, flip them over, and fry for about 1 minute more, until light golden brown on the other side as well. Using a slotted spoon, remove each beignet from the oil and drain thoroughly on paper towels. Repeat with the remaining beignets.

6. While still warm, toss the beignets in a bowl of confectioners' sugar, arrange on a platter, then shower with more confectioners' sugar.

Blackout Chocolate Doughnuts

 **DESCRIPTION** *These start with a baked soft, sweet, cakelike chocolate doughnut. Once cooled, the tops of the doughnuts are spread with a thick pudding and topped with a shower of crumbs created by crumbling a couple of the doughnuts.*

 **FIELD NOTES** *Ebinger's Blackout Cake was much beloved in the New York area until the bakery closed its doors in the early 1970s. No one knows the original recipe, but it featured a dark chocolate cake filled and frosted with a rich chocolate pudding, and then the entire cake was covered with dark chocolate cake crumbs. This is my doughnut version.*

 **LIFESPAN** *These will keep for up to 2 days in an airtight container in the refrigerator. Bring to room temperature before serving.*

Yield: *ten 3½-inch doughnuts*

INGREDIENTS

1 tablespoon sifted cornstarch
½ cup whole milk
¼ cup heavy cream
5 tablespoons sugar
1½ ounces unsweetened chocolate, such as Scharffen Berger 99%, Valrhona, or Callebaut, finely chopped

Pinch of salt
¼ teaspoon pure vanilla extract
1 recipe Baked Chocolate Doughnuts (page 21), baked and beginning to cool

DIRECTIONS

1. Place the cornstarch in a small bowl and drizzle a bit of the milk on top; whisk until smooth. Pour the remaining milk and the cream in a medium-size saucepan, then whisk in the cornstarch slurry, sugar, chocolate, and salt. Cook over medium-low heat, whisking often, until the chocolate melts, then watch carefully as you bring it to a gentle boil. Whisk often as it thickens and takes on a pudding-like consistency; it should simmer for 1 to 2 minutes. The pudding should be thick and glossy and the whisk should leave marks on top. Remove the pudding from the heat and whisk in the vanilla. Scrape into an airtight container and cool to warm room temperature. Press plastic wrap directly onto the surface (to keep a skin from forming), snap on the lid, and refrigerate for at least 6 hours or preferably overnight.

2. Crumble 2 of the baked doughnuts into a small bowl.

3. Using a small offset spatula, spread a generous amount of pudding on top of each doughnut. While the pudding is still moist, quickly and generously sprinkle the reserved crumbs on top.

Blueberry–Sour Cream Fritters

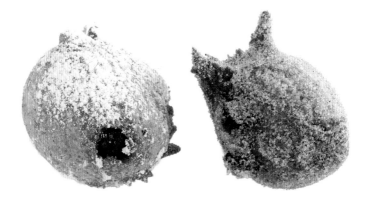

DESCRIPTION *This sweet, tender, rich fritter is filled with blueberries. Toss half in classic cinnamon sugar and half in a confectioners' sugar–cinnamon mixture.*

FIELD NOTE *This thick batter is dropped directly into hot oil. I use a #40 Zeroll ice cream scoop, which makes these fritters perfectly round. (The scoop measures 1⅞⁄₁₆ inches across.) Toss the fritters in the dry coatings while still warm.*

LIFESPAN *These are best eaten as soon as possible.*

Yield: *about 24 golf ball–size fritters*

INGREDIENTS

Toppings:
  Half a recipe Cinnamon-Sugar Topping
    (page 41)
  ½ cup sifted confectioners' sugar
  1 teaspoon ground cinnamon

Fritters:
  1 cup all-purpose flour
  1 cup sifted cake flour
  ½ teaspoon baking powder
  ½ teaspoon baking soda

½ teaspoon ground cinnamon
½ teaspoon salt
¾ cup full-fat sour cream
¾ cup granulated sugar
1 large egg, at room temperature
1½ teaspoons pure vanilla extract
¾ cup fresh or frozen (thawed and
  drained) blueberries
Flavorless vegetable oil for deep-frying,
  such as canola

DIRECTIONS

1. *For the toppings:* Place the cinnamon-sugar topping in a small bowl. Stir together the confectioners' sugar and cinnamon in another small bowl.

2. *For the fritters:* Whisk together both flours, the baking powder, baking soda, cinnamon, and salt in a large bowl to aerate and combine. Whisk together the sour cream, granulated sugar, egg, and vanilla in a medium-size bowl until smooth. Add the wet ingredients to the dry mixture and whisk gently until smooth.

3. Line a rimmed baking sheet pan with a triple layer of paper towels. Heat 3 inches of oil in a deep pot or deep-fat fryer to 350° to 355°F. When the oil is hot enough, use a 1 9⁄16-inch ice cream scoop to drop the batter (carefully) into

the oil. Alternatively, you can make small rounds by scooping up the batter with one tablespoon and scraping it off into the oil with another tablespoon. Fry a few fritters at a time; do not crowd. Fry until golden brown, about 1 minute and 10 seconds, flip them over, and fry for about 1 minute and 10 seconds more, until golden brown on the other side as well. Using a slotted spoon, remove each fritter from the oil and drain thoroughly on paper towels. Repeat with the remaining batter.

4. While they're still warm, roll half of the batch of fritters in the granulated sugar–cinnamon mixture and half of the batch in the confectioners' sugar–cinnamon mixture.

Boston Cream Doughnuts

DESCRIPTION *This soft yeast-raised doughnut is filled with vanilla pastry cream and covered with a chocolate glaze.*

FIELD NOTES *The classic dessert is called Boston cream pie, and yet it usually takes the form of a cake—two layers of yellow sponge cake, vanilla custard or pastry cream in the middle, and chocolate glaze on top. Those components rearranged as a doughnut are a classic at most doughnut shops. There will be leftover pastry cream; serve it with fresh fruit or make mini trifles.*

LIFESPAN *These are best eaten as soon as possible but will keep at room temperature for up to 2 hours.*

C

Yield: *about twenty-six 2½-inch filled doughnuts*

INGREDIENTS

1 recipe Krispy Kreme Kopykat Doughnuts (page 32) or Basic Yeast-Raised Doughnuts (page 28), prepared through the first rise

1 recipe Pastry Cream (page 42)

2 recipes Dark Chocolate Glaze (page 38)

Pastry bag and coupler fitted with a Bismarck #230 tip

DIRECTIONS

1. Generously flour two rimmed baking sheet pans. Gently punch down the dough and divide it in half. Roll out one piece of dough on a lightly floured work surface to ½-inch thickness. Cut out doughnuts with a lightly floured 2½-inch round cutter. Repeat with the remaining dough. Gently gather the scraps, press them together, roll out the dough, and cut out as many additional doughnuts as possible.

2. Place the doughnuts, well spaced, on the prepared pans. Let rise in a warm, draft-free location until doubled in size, about 30 minutes.

3. Line two rimmed baking sheet pans with a triple layer of paper towels. Heat 3 inches of oil in a deep pot or deep-fat fryer to 350° to 355°F. When the oil is hot enough, fry a few doughnuts at a time; do not crowd. Fry until light golden brown, about 1½ minutes, flip them over, and fry for about 1½ minutes more, until light golden brown on the other side as well. Using a slotted spoon, remove each doughnut from the oil and drain thoroughly on paper towels. Repeat with the remaining doughnuts. Cool thoroughly.

4. Scrape the pastry cream into the pastry bag. Insert the tip into the side of a doughnut. Squeeze the pastry bag and fill the doughnut with pastry cream just until the center of the doughnut slightly bulges. (You are aiming to pipe a generous 2 to 3 teaspoons of filling inside.) Repeat with the remaining doughnuts and pastry cream.

5. Dip the top of each doughnut in the glaze and let sit for about 5 minutes to allow the glaze to set.

Browned Butter–Brown Sugar
Sour Cream Doughnuts

DESCRIPTION *This very moist doughnut is made with dark brown sugar and browned butter for an incomparable toffee-like flavor. The browned butter frosting accents the flavors further.*

FIELD NOTES *Dark brown sugar, as opposed to light brown, is necessary to achieve the desired depth of flavor. Browning butter is easy; you simply melt it until it develops a nutty brown color and aroma, taking care not to burn it. The butter reduces a bit during this process, so the ingredient list requires more butter than is used in the recipe. Measure carefully in a small liquid measuring cup for the actual amount needed. Note that the color of the glaze is a tad beige and might not be what you expect. The flavor is so excellent that I forgive its odd look.*

LIFESPAN *These are best eaten as soon as possible.*

Yield: *about twelve 3-inch doughnuts*

INGREDIENTS

Doughnuts:

7 tablespoons unsalted butter
2½ cups all-purpose flour
1 cup sifted cake flour
1 tablespoon baking powder
1 teaspoon salt
½ teaspoon baking soda
1 cup firmly packed dark brown sugar
2 large eggs, at room temperature
1½ teaspoons pure vanilla extract
1 cup full-fat sour cream, at room
  temperature
½ teaspoon freshly grated nutmeg
Flavorless vegetable oil for deep-frying,
  such as canola

Browned butter frosting:

½ cup (1 stick) unsalted butter, at room
  temperature
1 cup sifted confectioners' sugar
Pinch of salt, or to taste

DIRECTIONS

1. *For the doughnuts*: Melt the butter in a small saucepan over medium heat until it turns deep amber brown; don't let it burn. Measure out 5 tablespoons, which you'll need for the recipe; set aside. (If you have any left over, save for another purpose.)

2. Whisk together both flours, the baking powder, salt, and baking soda in a medium-size bowl to aerate and combine.

3. In a large bowl, beat together the brown sugar and eggs with an electric mixer until pale and creamy, or whisk well by hand. Beat in the reserved browned butter, vanilla, sour cream, and nutmeg until combined. Add the dry mixture in two batches and stir with a wooden spoon just until the dough comes together. Refrigerate for at least 2 hours or up to overnight.

4. Remove the dough from the refrigerator. Line a rimmed baking sheet pan with a triple layer of paper towels. Heat 3 inches of oil in a deep pot or deep-fat fryer to 350° to 355°F.

5. While the oil is heating, dust the work surface with flour. Scrape the dough onto the surface, dust the top of the dough lightly with flour, and roll out to ½-inch thickness. Cut out doughnuts with a lightly floured 3-inch round cutter. Gently gather the scraps, press them together, roll out the dough, and cut out as many additional doughnuts as possible.

6. Fry a few doughnuts at a time; do not crowd. Fry until light golden brown, about 1 minute and 15 seconds, flip them over, and fry for about 1 minute and 15 seconds more, until light golden brown on the other side as well. Using a slotted spoon, remove each doughnut from the oil and drain thoroughly on paper towels. Repeat with the remaining dough.

7. *For the frosting*: Melt the butter in a small saucepan over medium heat until it turns deep amber brown; don't let it burn. Place the confectioners' sugar in a medium-size bowl. Whisk in the browned butter until the glaze is perfectly smooth. Add a pinch of salt, taste, and adjust as desired. Drizzle the frosting over the cooled doughnuts using a parchment paper cone, fork, or spoon.

Buttercream-Filled Doughnuts

DESCRIPTION *Buttercream doughnuts are very popular in doughnut shops and for good reason: They combine a chewy, yeasty doughnut shell with a sweet vanilla buttercream center. This is heaven for those with a serious sweet tooth. I have bolstered the vanilla flavor by using both vanilla bean and vanilla extract. I finish these off with a toss in confectioners' sugar. If you're a chocolate lover, don't miss the variation on page 64 for chocolate buttercream–filled doughnuts topped with cocoa glaze.*

FIELD NOTES *Vanilla beans are expensive, so get your money's worth. They should be moist and flexible, and once you have scraped out the tiny seeds from within the beans, bury the bean pieces in 4 cups of granulated sugar to create vanilla sugar for future use.*

LIFESPAN *These are best eaten as soon as possible.*

C

Yield: *about twenty-six 2½-inch filled doughnuts*

INGREDIENTS

1 recipe Krispy Kreme Kopykat Doughnuts (page 32) or Basic Yeast-Raised Doughnuts (page 28), prepared through the first rise

Buttercream:

¾ cup (1½ sticks) unsalted butter, at room temperature, cut into pieces

6 ⅔ cups sifted confectioners' sugar

1 teaspoon pure vanilla extract

1 plump, moist vanilla bean

¼ to ½ cup whole milk, at room temperature

Confectioners' sugar

Pastry bag and coupler fitted with a Bismarck #230 tip

DIRECTIONS

1. Generously flour two rimmed baking sheet pans. Gently punch down the dough and divide it in half. Roll out one piece of dough on a lightly floured work surface to ½-inch thickness. Cut out doughnuts with a lightly floured 2½-inch round cutter. Repeat with the remaining dough. Gently gather the scraps, press them together, roll out the dough, and cut out as many additional doughnuts as possible. Place doughnuts, well spaced, on the prepared pans. Let rise in a warm, draft-free location until doubled in size, about 30 minutes.

2. While the doughnuts are rising, prepare the buttercream. In a large bowl, beat the butter with an electric mixer on medium-high speed until creamy, about 2 minutes. Add 1 cup of the confectioners' sugar and the vanilla extract and beat until light and fluffy, about 3 minutes, scraping down the sides of the bowl once or twice. Slit the vanilla bean lengthwise and use a butter knife or teaspoon to scrape all of the tiny seeds into the frosting. Beat again to begin incorporating the seeds. Add

the remaining 5⅔ cups confectioners' sugar and ¼ cup of the milk, beating on high speed until the buttercream is silky smooth. The frosting should be soft enough so that it will flow easily through the piping tip. Keep thinning out with additional milk, one teaspoon at a time, if needed to achieve this soft texture.

3. Line two rimmed baking sheet pans with a triple layer of paper towels. Heat 3 inches of oil in a deep pot or deep-fat fryer to 350° to 355°F. When the oil is hot enough, fry a few doughnuts at a time; do not crowd. Fry until light golden brown, about 1½ minutes, flip them over, and fry for about 1½ minutes more, until light golden brown on the other side as well. Using a slotted spoon, remove each doughnut from the oil and drain thoroughly on paper towels. Repeat with the remaining doughnuts. Cool until just barely warm to the touch.

4. Scrape the buttercream into the pastry bag. Insert the tip into the side of a doughnut. Squeeze the pastry bag and

fill the doughnut with buttercream just until the center of the doughnut slightly bulges. (You are aiming to pipe a generous 2 to 3 teaspoons of filling inside.) Repeat with the remaining doughnuts and pastry cream.

5. Toss the filled doughnuts in confectioners' sugar to coat completely.

VARIATION

For Chocolate Buttercream–Filled Doughnuts, finely chop 4 ounces semisweet chocolate (such as Callebaut or Ghirardelli), then melt it gently and whisk until smooth. Prepare the vanilla buttercream as above, but use only ½ teaspoon pure vanilla extract and omit the vanilla bean. Beat the chocolate into the buttercream along with the milk. Fill the doughnuts as directed above, and then prepare 2 recipes Cocoa Glaze (page 37). Dip the top of each doughnut in the glaze and let sit for about 5 minutes to allow the glaze to set.

Cappuccino Doughnuts with Espresso Cream Filling

 **DESCRIPTION** *This yeast-raised dough is made with milk, yielding a flavorful and tender casing for an espresso custard filling. Cocoa and cinnamon on top complete the cappuccino picture.*

 **FIELD NOTES** *Note that the custard filling can be made 2 days ahead, and the dough was formulated to rest in the refrigerator overnight, both of which are time savers. Use true espresso powder, as opposed to instant coffee, for that deep, rich espresso flavor.*

 **LIFESPAN** *These are best eaten as soon as possible but will keep at room temperature for up to 2 hours.*

Yield: *about twenty-four 2½-inch filled doughnuts*

INGREDIENTS

Espresso cream filling:
½ cup sugar
6 tablespoons all-purpose flour
2 tablespoons instant espresso powder
2 cups whole milk, at room temperature
5 large egg yolks, at room temperature
Pinch of salt
2 tablespoons unsalted butter
1 teaspoon pure vanilla extract

Doughnuts:
1 cup plus 2 tablespoons warm whole milk
  (110° to 115°F)
One 0.25-ounce package active dry yeast
4 cups all-purpose flour
¼ cup sugar

1 teaspoon ground cinnamon
½ teaspoon salt
10 tablespoons (1¼ sticks) unsalted butter,
  melted and cooled to lukewarm
2 large eggs, at room temperature
Flavorless vegetable oil for deep-frying,
  such as canola

Topping:
½ cup sugar
2 teaspoons Dutch-processed cocoa
  powder
2 teaspoons ground cinnamon

Pastry bag and coupler fitted with a
  Bismarck #230 tip

DIRECTIONS

1. *For the filling*: Whisk together the sugar, flour, and espresso powder in a heavy medium-size saucepan. Gradually whisk in the milk until smooth, then whisk in the egg yolks and salt. Add the butter. Cook over medium-high heat until the mixture thickens and gently boils, whisking constantly, about 6 minutes. Whisk in the vanilla. Transfer to a storage container. Press plastic wrap directly onto the surface (to keep a skin from forming). Chill until cold, at least 6 hours and up to 2 days.

2. *For the doughnuts*: Place the warm milk in a large bowl and sprinkle the yeast over it. Stir to combine and let sit for 5 minutes. Whisk together the flour, sugar, cinnamon, and salt in a medium-size bowl to aerate and combine. Whisk together the melted butter and eggs in a separate bowl until combined.

3. Whisk the egg mixture into the yeast mixture by hand or use the dough hook of a stand mixer. Beat in the flour mixture about ½ cup at a time, beating until the dough is smooth and beginning to pull away from the sides of the bowl, about 5 minutes. Scrape the dough from the hook, if using. Let the dough rest for 5 minutes. Scrape the dough into a buttered bowl (the dough will be sticky), making sure there is plenty of headroom. Cover the bowl with plastic wrap and refrigerate overnight.

4. Generously flour two rimmed baking sheet pans. Gently punch down the dough and divide it in half. Roll out one piece of dough on a lightly floured work surface to ⅓-inch thickness. Cut out doughnuts with a lightly floured 2½-inch round cutter. Repeat with the remaining dough. Gently gather the scraps, press them together, roll out the dough, and cut out as many additional doughnuts as possible.

5. Place the doughnuts, well spaced, on the prepared pans. Let rise in a warm, draft-free location until doubled in size, about 1 hour.

6. Line two rimmed baking sheet pans with a triple layer of paper towels. Heat 3 inches of oil in a deep pot or deep-fat fryer to 350° to 355°F.

7. While the oil is heating, make the topping by whisking together the sugar, cocoa, and cinnamon in a wide shallow bowl.

8. Fry a few doughnuts at a time; do not crowd. Fry until light golden brown, about 1 minute and 15 seconds, flip them over, and fry for about 1 minute and 15 seconds more, until light golden brown on the other side as well. Using a slotted spoon, remove each doughnut from the oil and drain thoroughly on paper towels. Repeat with the remaining doughnuts.

9. Roll each doughnut on all sides in the topping while they are still slightly warm. Let the doughnuts cool on racks that have been cleared of used paper towels.

10. Scrape the filling into the pastry bag. Insert the tip into the side of a doughnut. Squeeze the pastry bag and fill the doughnut with custard just until the center of the doughnut slightly bulges. (You are aiming to pipe a generous 2 to 3 teaspoons of filling inside.) Repeat with the remaining doughnuts and filling.

Caramel-Bourbon-Pecan Doughnuts

DESCRIPTION *This doughnut features a sticky, crunchy topping combining caramel and pecans with a nice hit of bourbon. Try this on your favorite cake-style doughnuts or one of the recommendations that follow.*

FIELD NOTES *As I was researching everything doughnut related, I came across a Food Network episode of* Throwdown with Bobby Flay *where he challenged Mark Israel from the Doughnut Plant. Bobby prepared a topping similar to this one—and won the challenge! If you like gooey, nutty textures and flavors, you will love this. The bourbon flavor is pronounced; you may halve the alcohol if you like. Any extra glaze is fabulous warmed up and poured over ice cream.*

LIFESPAN *These are best eaten as soon as possible.*

Yield: *depends on doughnut recipe chosen; glaze recipe makes enough to coat twenty-four 3-inch doughnuts*

INGREDIENTS

Caramel-Bourbon-Pecan Glaze:
2¼ cups sugar
⅔ cup water
1½ cups heavy cream, at room
  temperature
3 tablespoons unsalted butter, at room
  temperature
3 tablespoons bourbon
1½ teaspoons pure vanilla extract

Heaping ¼ teaspoon salt
Scant 1 cup pecan halves, toasted (page 10)
  and finely chopped

1 recipe Sour Cream Doughnuts (page 24),
  Old-Fashioned Buttermilk Doughnuts
  (page 22), or Chocolate Cake-Style
  Doughnuts (page 26), cut into 3-inch
  rings, fried, and beginning to cool

DIRECTIONS

1. Stir the sugar and water together in a deep pot (you need headroom, as it will bubble up furiously when the cream is added). Bring to a simmer over medium-high heat, swirling the pan once or twice, but do not stir. Cook until the sugar is caramelized and has turned a dark golden brown. Remove from the heat and add the cream; the mixture will bubble vigorously. After the bubbling subsides, place the pan back on the burner over low heat. Add the butter and bourbon and whisk just until smooth. Remove from the heat and whisk in the vanilla, salt, and nuts. Pour the glaze into a heatproof bowl and cool until slightly thickened.

2. Line two rimmed baking sheet pans with aluminum foil or parchment paper. Dip the tops of the doughnuts into the glaze or spread it on top using a small offset spatula. Let the glazed doughnuts sit on the prepared pans until the glaze sets, 5 to 10 minutes.

Carrot Cake Doughnuts

● **DESCRIPTION** *This is carrot cake in a doughnut form—carrots, spices, brown sugar, raisins, and nuts. Keep it classic and top with Cream Cheese Frosting.*

● **FIELD NOTES** *The carrots are shredded and folded into the batter, just as they are for classic carrot cake, but here I have also added some mashed cooked carrots for extra moisture, color, and flavor. Simply peel and thinly slice 4 large carrots, cover with water, boil until tender, drain, then process until smooth in a food processor fitted with a metal blade.*

● **LIFESPAN** *These are best eaten as soon as possible.*

Yield: *about sixteen 3-inch doughnuts*

INGREDIENTS

3 cups all-purpose flour
½ cup sifted cake flour
1 tablespoon plus 1 teaspoon baking powder
1½ teaspoons ground cinnamon
1 teaspoon baking soda
½ teaspoon freshly grated nutmeg
½ teaspoon salt
½ cup dark raisins, chopped
¼ cup walnut halves, finely chopped

1 cup firmly packed light brown sugar
2 large eggs, at room temperature
1 cup mashed cooked carrots (see Field Notes)
1 cup finely shredded raw carrots
¼ cup (½ stick) unsalted butter, melted and cooled
2 tablespoons flavorless vegetable oil, such as canola, plus more for deep-frying
1 recipe Cream Cheese Frosting (page 41)

DIRECTIONS

1. Whisk together both flours, the baking powder, cinnamon, baking soda, nutmeg, and salt in a medium-size bowl to aerate and combine. Toss in the raisins and nuts.

2. In a large bowl, beat together the brown sugar and eggs with an electric mixer until pale and creamy, or whisk well by hand. Beat in the cooked carrots, shredded carrots, melted butter, and 2 tablespoons oil until combined. Add the dry mixture in two batches and stir with a wooden spoon just until the dough comes together. Cover and refrigerate for at least 1 hour or up to overnight.

3. Remove the dough from the refrigerator. Line a rimmed baking sheet pan with a triple layer of paper towels; set aside. Prepare a deep pot or deep-fat fryer. Heat 3 inches of oil to 350° to 355°F.

4. While the oil is heating, dust the work surface generously with flour. Scrape the dough onto the surface, dust the top of the dough lightly with flour, and roll out to ½-inch thickness. Cut out doughnuts with a lightly floured 3-inch round cutter. Gently gather the scraps, press them together, roll out the dough, and cut out as many additional doughnuts as possible.

5. Fry a few doughnuts at a time; do not crowd. Fry until light golden brown, about 1½ minutes, flip them over, and fry for about 1½ minutes more, until light golden brown on the other side as well. Using a slotted spoon, remove each doughnut from the oil and drain thoroughly on paper towels. Repeat with the remaining doughnuts.

6. While the doughnuts are still barely warm, spread the tops with the frosting using a small offset spatula.

Cereal Killer (aka Fiber None) Doughnuts

DESCRIPTION *This ring-shaped yeast-raised doughnut is covered with a thick vanilla frosting and topped with your choice of cereal, such as Cap'n Crunch, Froot Loops, Honey Smacks, or whatever you like.*

FIELD NOTES *Voodoo Doughnut (voodoodonut.com) in Portland, Oregon, is a destination bakery for doughnut lovers, and as far as I know, they came up with this idea. The doughnuts are colorful, crunchy, and can be tailored to your taste, depending on the cereal chosen. The "aka Fiber None" suggestion came from my online pal "beachgirl"—she has a great sense of humor and came up with a great name for a great doughnut. Have fun with these.*

LIFESPAN *These are best eaten as soon as possible.*

Yield: *about twenty-four 3-inch doughnuts*

INGREDIENTS

1 recipe Krispy Kreme Kopykat Doughnuts (page 32) or Basic Yeast-Raised Doughnuts (page 28), cut into 3-inch rings, fried, and beginning to cool

1 recipe Buttercream (page 63)
Breakfast cereal of your choice

DIRECTIONS

While the doughnuts are still warm, spread the buttercream on the tops using a small offset spatula. Gently but firmly press your choice of cereal into the frosting, covering the doughnut. Let sit for about 5 minutes to allow the frosting to set.

Cheesecake-Filled
Raised Doughnuts

 **DESCRIPTION** *A refrigerator-style cheesecake filling is lightened with cream, flavored with vanilla, gently sweetened, and piped into cooled yeast-raised doughnuts. I like to finish these off very simply with a toss in confectioners' sugar.*

FIELD NOTES *Make sure to cool the doughnuts before filling them, as you should do with any dairy-based filling.*

LIFESPAN *These are best eaten as soon as possible (for health and safety reasons) but will keep at room temperature up to 1 hour.*

Yield: *about twenty-six 2½-inch filled doughnuts*

INGREDIENTS

1 recipe Krispy Kreme Kopykat Doughnuts
(page 32) or Basic Yeast-Raised
Doughnuts (page 28), cut into 2½-inch
rounds, fried, and beginning to cool
Sifted confectioners' sugar

Cheesecake filling:

One 8-ounce package cream cheese, at
room temperature, cut into pieces

1 cup heavy cream, plus more as needed
¼ cup granulated sugar
1 teaspoon freshly squeezed lemon juice
¼ teaspoon pure vanilla extract

Pastry bag and coupler fitted with a
Bismarck #230 tip

DIRECTIONS

1. While they are still slightly warm, roll
the doughnuts on all sides in the confectioners' sugar. Let the doughnuts
cool on racks that have been cleared of
used paper towels.

2. *For the cheesecake filling:* In a medium-
size bowl, beat the cream cheese with
an electric mixer until very smooth and
creamy. Add the cream and beat on
high speed until combined and smooth.
The cream will thicken and the entire
mixture will have a thick consistency.
Add the granulated sugar and beat
until it dissolves and the mixture is
thick and has a smooth, creamy body.

Beat in the lemon juice and vanilla. The
mixture should be the right consistency
to be able to be piped through a pastry tip. If it is too thick, beat in more
cream, 1 teaspoon at a time.

3. Scrape the cheesecake filling into the
pastry bag. Insert the tip into the side
of a cooled doughnut. Squeeze the
pastry bag and fill the doughnut with
pastry cream just until the center of
the doughnut slightly bulges. (You are
aiming to pipe a generous 2 to 3 teaspoons of filling inside.) Repeat with
the remaining doughnuts and filling.

Chocolate Chip Ganache-Glazed Baked Doughnuts

 **DESCRIPTION** *The basic recipe for baked doughnuts is prepared with miniature semisweet chocolate morsels added to the batter. Dark Chocolate Ganache Glaze is spread on the doughnuts and more chocolate morsels are scattered on top, providing a great contrast between the springy doughnut and the crunch of mini chips.*

 **FIELD NOTES** *This is a very easy recipe to make, and if you have only one of the Norpro Doughnut Pans, you can halve the recipe for a 6-doughnut yield.*

 **LIFESPAN** *These are best eaten the day they are made.*

⊕ ☺

Yield: *twelve 3½-inch doughnuts*

⊘ INGREDIENTS

1 recipe Baked Doughnuts (page 20), prepared with ½ cup miniature semisweet chocolate morsels folded into the final batter, baked, and cooled

¼ cup miniature semisweet chocolate morsels

Half a recipe Dark Chocolate Ganache Glaze (page 39)

⊘ DIRECTIONS

Spread the glaze on the tops of the cooled doughnuts using a small offset spatula. Sprinkle the chocolate morsels on top of the glaze while it is still moist. Refrigerate briefly to set the ganache and help the morsels adhere.

Chocolate-Coconut Doughnuts

DESCRIPTION *This recipe gives you all of the flavors of a Mounds candy bar in a doughnut. Coconut–Sour Cream Doughnuts are covered with chocolate-coconut ganache, with additional coconut sprinkled on top as the crowning glory.*

FIELD NOTES *Make sure to use pure unsweetened coconut milk and not cream of coconut, which has a very high sugar content.*

LIFESPAN *These are best eaten the day they are made.*

Yield: *fourteen 3-inch doughnuts*

INGREDIENTS

Chocolate-coconut ganache:
- 1 cup pure unsweetened coconut milk
- 10 ounces semisweet or bittersweet chocolate (50% to 64% cacao), such as Valrhona Equatoriale, Callebaut, or Ghirardelli, finely chopped
- 1 tablespoon unsalted butter, at room temperature

- 1 recipe Coconut–Sour Cream Doughnuts (page 24), cut into 3-inch rings, fried, and beginning to cool
- 1⅔ cups lightly packed sweetened long-shred coconut

DIRECTIONS

1. *For the ganache*: Bring the coconut milk to a simmer over medium heat in a 2-quart wide saucepan. Remove from the heat and immediately sprinkle the chocolate into the cream. Cover and let sit for 5 minutes. Gently stir the ganache until smooth—the heat of the cream should melt the chocolate. If the chocolate does not melt completely, place the pan over very low heat and stir the ganache often, until melted, taking care not to burn it. Stir or whisk in the butter until melted and incorpo- rated. Cool until warm but still fluid. The ganache is ready to use, or you may refrigerate it in an airtight con- tainer for up to 1 week. (If refrigerated, heat gently in the microwave or on the stovetop until fluid before proceeding.)

2. While the doughnuts are still warm, dip the tops in the ganache. Sprinkle the shredded coconut on top of the ganache while it is still wet. Let sit for about 5 minutes to allow the ganache to set.

Chocolate-Covered Strawberry Doughnuts

DESCRIPTION *Chocolate Yeast-Raised Doughnuts are filled with strawberry preserves and topped with a dark chocolate ganache glaze.*

FIELD NOTES *Whole Foods Market and some specialty stores carry freeze-dried fruit made by a company called Just Tomatoes! The strawberries are bright red and packed with flavor. It's a pricey product, but a few pieces of the sliced berries on top of these doughnuts will really punch up the strawberry flavor.*

LIFESPAN *These are best eaten as soon as possible.*

Yield: *about twenty-four 2½-inch filled doughnuts*

INGREDIENTS

1 recipe Chocolate Yeast-Raised
Doughnuts (page 30), prepared through
the first rise
1½ cups strawberry preserves
Flavorless vegetable oil for deep-frying,
such as canola

1½ recipes Dark Chocolate Ganache Glaze
(page 39)
One 2-ounce package (about 2 cups)
freeze-dried strawberries (optional)

DIRECTIONS

1. Generously flour two rimmed baking sheet pans. Gently punch down the dough and divide it in half. Roll out one piece of dough on a lightly floured work surface to ¼-inch thickness. Cut out dough rounds with a lightly floured 2½-inch round cutter. Repeat with the remaining dough. Gently gather the scraps, press them together, roll out the dough, and cut out as many additional rounds as possible. Make sure you end up with an even number.

2. Using two cereal spoons, dollop about 2 teaspoons of strawberry preserves in the centers of half of the dough rounds. Dip a pastry brush in room-temperature water and lightly brush the edges of the dough around the preserves. Place a plain round on top of each filled round and press the edges together with your fingertips to seal them well.

3. Place the doughnuts, well spaced, on the prepared pans. Let rise in a warm, draft-free location until doubled in size, about 30 minutes.

4. Line a rimmed baking sheet pan with a triple layer of paper towels. Heat 3 inches of oil in a deep pot or deep-fat fryer to 350° to 355°F. When the oil is hot enough, fry a few doughnuts at a time; do not crowd. Fry until light golden brown, about 1½ minutes, flip them over, and fry for about 1½ minutes more, until light golden brown on the other side as well. Using a slotted spoon, remove each doughnut from the oil and drain thoroughly on paper towels. Repeat with the remaining doughnuts.

5. While the doughnuts are still warm, dip the tops in the glaze and place a few slices of freeze-dried strawberries, if using, on top of the glaze while it is still wet. Let sit for about 5 minutes to allow the ganache to set.

Chocolate Mousse Doughnuts

 **DESCRIPTION** *These yeast-raised doughnuts are filled with fluffy chocolate mousse and covered with a chocolate glaze.*

 **FIELD NOTES** *The chocolate mousse can be made a day ahead and should be kept refrigerated until right before serving. Don't be afraid of whisking the egg white and the cream by hand; there is just one egg and a very small amount of cream and they whip up quickly. Pipe the mousse into the doughnuts within an hour of serving. The mousse is made with uncooked eggs, so be sure your eggs come from a reliable source and have no cracks; avoid the recipe if you or lyour guests have a compromised immune system. By the way, it is just as easy to whip double the amount of egg whites and cream; if you double the recipe, you can have extra mousse to serve for dessert.*

 **LIFESPAN** *These are best eaten as soon as possible but will keep at room temperature up to 2 hours.*

Yield: *about twenty-eight 2½-inch filled doughnuts*

INGREDIENTS

Chocolate mousse:

2 ounces semisweet or bittersweet chocolate (not more than 60% cacao), such as Callebaut or Ghirardelli, finely chopped

1 tablespoon unsalted butter

1 large egg, separated

Pinch of cream of tartar

1 tablespoon sugar

¼ cup heavy cream, chilled

⅛ teaspoon pure vanilla extract

1 recipe Krispy Kreme Kopykat Doughnuts (page 32) or Basic Yeast-Raised Doughnuts (page 28), cut into 2½-inch rounds, fried, and cooled

2 recipes Cocoa Glaze (page 37) or Dark Chocolate Glaze (page 38)

Pastry bag and coupler fitted with a Bismarck #230 tip

DIRECTIONS

1. *For the mousse*: Melt the chocolate and butter together in a microwave or the top of a double boiler over simmering water; stir until smooth. Remove from the heat and cool slightly. Scrape the mixture into a medium-size bowl (or microwave it in a medium-size bowl to begin with). Whisk in the egg yolk.

2. Whisk the egg white in a clean, grease-free bowl with a large balloon whisk until frothy; whisk in the cream of tartar until soft peaks form. Sprinkle the sugar over the top and whip until stiff peaks form. Fold about half of the egg white into the chocolate mixture to lighten, then fold in the remainder until just a few streaks of white remain. Wash and dry the whisk well.

3. Whisk together the cream and vanilla in a small bowl until soft peaks form. Fold the cream into the chocolate mousse until no streaks remain. Cover the bowl and refrigerate until firm, at least 4 hours or up to overnight.

4. Scrape the chilled mousse into the pastry bag. Insert the tip into the side of a cooled doughnut. Squeeze the pastry bag and fill the doughnut with mousse just until the center of the doughnut slightly bulges. (You are aiming to pipe a generous 2 to 3 teaspoons of filling inside.) Repeat with the remaining doughnuts and mousse.

5. Dip the tops of the doughnuts in the glaze and let sit for about 5 minutes to allow the glaze to set.

Chocolate–Salted Caramel Doughnuts

 **DESCRIPTION** *If you make only one doughnut in this book and you are a chocolate person, this is the one to try—chocolate cake doughnuts dipped in a very dark caramel glaze, covered with shards of dark chocolate and a sprinkling of* fleur de sel.

 **FIELD NOTES** *When making the caramel, be sure to cook it until it is very dark (but not burnt) for a very deep caramel flavor. It tastes fabulous over ice cream, too. Also make sure the caramel has cooled on the doughnuts before sprinkling with the chocolate shavings or they will melt. The amount of salt is up to you, but just a few grains on each doughnut will do the trick. Regular table salt will not do;* fleur de sel *retains its shape and crunch, and that is part of the overall charm of this doughnut.*

 **LIFESPAN** *These are best eaten as soon as possible.*

Yield: *about fourteen 3-inch doughnuts*

INGREDIENTS

One 6-ounce block bittersweet or
semisweet chocolate, such as Valrhona
Caraque, Caraïbe, Extra Bitter, or
Equatoriale, or Callebaut

Caramel glaze:
2 cups sugar
½ cup water
1 cup heavy cream, at room temperature

1 recipe Chocolate Cake-Style Doughnuts
(page 26), cut into 3-inch rings, fried, and
beginning to cool
Fleur de sel

DIRECTIONS

1. Use a sharp vegetable peeler to shave small curls off the block of chocolate directly into an airtight plastic container. These may be made a few days ahead and refrigerated.

2. *For the glaze*: Combine the sugar and water in a deep medium-size saucepan. Stir over medium heat until the sugar dissolves. Increase the heat and boil without stirring, occasionally brushing down the sides of the pan with a wet pastry brush. Watch carefully for the moment when the sugar syrup just begins to color, which could be anywhere from 5 to 10 minutes after it comes to a boil. The time is not important; pay attention to the color. Watch constantly at this point, as the color will develop quickly, changing from pale gold to rich amber. Continue boiling and within a minute it will darken to a rich reddish brown, the color of a pecan. Immediately remove the pan from the heat. Slowly pour the cream over the caramel. It will bubble up; just allow it to bubble and then subside. Whisk gently until smooth. If the caramel hardens, place the pan back over low heat and whisk gently until smooth. Pour the glaze into a heatproof bowl and cool until slightly thickened.

3. Line two rimmed baking sheet pans with aluminum foil or parchment paper and coat with nonstick cooking spray.

4. While the doughnuts are still warm, dip the tops in the glaze or spread it using a small offset spatula. Let the doughnuts sit on the prepared pans until the glaze begins to cool. Sprinkle generously with dark chocolate curls while the glaze is cool but still a bit sticky. Sprinkle with a few grains of salt.

Chocolate–Sour Cream Doughnuts

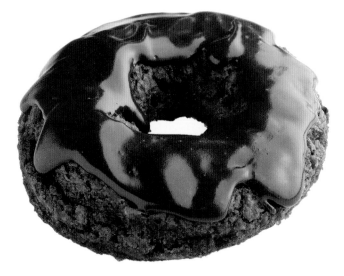

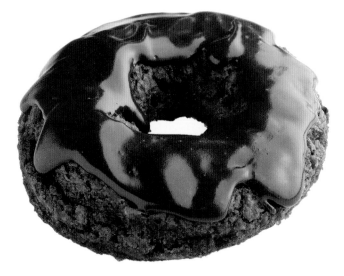 **DESCRIPTION** *These cake-style doughnuts have a rich, moist texture courtesy of the sour cream and a dark chocolate flavor from Dutch-processed cocoa.*

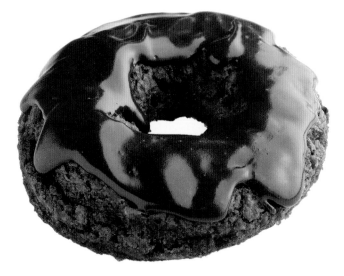 **FIELD NOTES** *I tested a slew of chocolate cake-style doughnuts, and many of the recipes came out dry, even those from respected cookbooks. I have brought you only the ones that will truly satisfy. Sour cream adds moistness to the batter and, while very rich, it makes for a fabulous chocolate cake doughnut. Chocolate doughnuts are so dark that it is hard to tell when they are done, so frying a sample doughnut is a must. Try these topped with Mocha Glaze (page 38).*

 LIFESPAN *These are best eaten as soon as possible.*

Yield: *about twelve 3-inch doughnuts*

INGREDIENTS

1¾ cups all-purpose flour
1 cup sifted cake flour
⅓ cup sifted Dutch-processed cocoa
  powder
1 tablespoon baking powder
½ teaspoon baking soda
1 teaspoon salt
1 cup plus 2 tablespoons sugar

2 large eggs, at room temperature
1 cup full-fat sour cream, at room
  temperature
5 tablespoons unsalted butter, melted and
  cooled
2 teaspoons pure vanilla extract
Flavorless vegetable oil for deep-frying,
  such as canola

DIRECTIONS

1. Whisk together both flours, the cocoa, baking powder, baking soda, and salt in a medium-size bowl to aerate and combine.

2. In a large bowl, beat together the sugar and eggs with an electric mixer until pale and creamy, or whisk well by hand. Beat in the sour cream, melted butter, and vanilla until combined. Add the dry mixture in two batches and stir with a wooden spoon just until the dough comes together. Cover and refrigerate for at least 2 hours or up to overnight.

3. Remove the dough from the refrigerator. Line a rimmed baking sheet pan with a triple layer of paper towels. Heat 3 inches of oil in a deep pot or deep-fat fryer to 350° to 355°F.

4. While the oil is heating, dust a work surface with flour. Scrape the chilled dough onto the surface, dust the top of the dough lightly with flour, and roll out to ½-inch thickness. Cut out doughnuts with a lightly floured 3-inch round cutter. Gently gather the scraps, press them together, roll out the dough, and cut out as many additional doughnuts as possible.

5. Fry a few doughnuts at a time; do not crowd. Fry about 1½ minutes, flip them over, and fry for about 1½ minutes more, until just cooked through. Using a slotted spoon, remove each doughnut from the oil and drain thoroughly on paper towels. Repeat with the remaining dough.

Churros with
Chocolate Dipping Sauce

DESCRIPTION *These ridged strips are made from* pâte à choux *(cream puff) dough, piped out of a pastry bag fitted with a star tip directly into the hot oil. The ridges created by the star tip allow the cinnamon sugar coating to cling to a large surface area, which is part of their charm. They are light, crisp, and very easy to make. The chocolate dipping sauce is optional, but a very nice addition.*

FIELD NOTES *Churros and similar pastries are found in Spain and Mexico as well as other Latin American countries. Sometimes sold by street vendors, they are a popular breakfast treat. They are often served with hot chocolate or with a thick, almost pudding-like chocolate for dipping, as I have included here. The dipping sauce is made first so that it is ready to serve when the churros are still warm. (The sauce might develop a bit of a skin; simply whisk until smooth before serving.)*

LIFESPAN *These are best eaten as soon as possible.*

© 🕐 ☺

Yield: *about 36 churros*

INGREDIENTS

Chocolate sauce:
4 ounces semisweet chocolate, such as
  Callebaut or Ghirardelli, finely chopped
2 cups whole milk
1 tablespoon cornstarch

Churros:
1 cup water
6 tablespoons (¾ stick) unsalted butter, cut
  into pieces
1 teaspoon sugar
½ teaspoon salt

1 cup all-purpose flour
3 large eggs, at room temperature
½ teaspoon pure vanilla extract
⅛ teaspoon ground cinnamon
Flavorless vegetable oil for deep-frying,
  such as canola

Half a recipe Cinnamon-Sugar Topping
(page 41)

Pastry bag fitted with a large star tip (about
½-inch opening), such as Ateco #847

DIRECTIONS

1. *For the chocolate sauce*: Place the chocolate and 1 cup of the milk in a small, heavy saucepan over low heat. Cook, whisking frequently, until the chocolate is melted and smooth. Meanwhile, whisk the remaining 1 cup milk with the cornstarch in a small bowl to dissolve the cornstarch, then whisk it into the hot chocolate mixture. Bring to a gentle boil, whisking constantly, and boil until the mixture has thickened, 1 to 2 minutes. Remove from the heat and keep warm.

2. *For the churros*: Combine the water, butter, sugar, and salt in a medium-size saucepan. Bring to a rolling boil over medium-high heat and immediately remove from the heat. Quickly stir in the flour all at once with a wooden spoon, until the dough comes together. Place over very low heat and keep stirring to dry out the dough, about 1 minute. It should come away cleanly from the sides of the saucepan. Scrape it into the bowl of a stand mixer fitted with a paddle attachment. Turn on medium speed and add the eggs one at a time, allowing each egg to be absorbed before

continuing. Beat in the vanilla and cinnamon. The batter should be smooth, golden yellow, and firm enough to hold a shape when mounded with a spoon.

3. Place the cinnamon-sugar topping in a shallow bowl. Line two rimmed baking sheet pans with a triple layer of paper towels. Scrape dough into pastry bag.

4. Heat 3 inches of oil in a deep pot or deep-fat fryer to 350° to 355°F. When the oil is hot enough, pipe 5-inch-long strips of dough directly into the hot oil, cutting the dough with a scissor or knife to release it from the tip. Fry a few at a time; do not crowd. Fry until golden brown, about 1 minute, flip over, and fry for about 1 minute more, until golden brown on the other side. Using a slotted spoon, remove each churro from the oil, place on paper towels for a moment, then immediately roll in the cinnamon sugar, tossing to coat completely. Transfer to a serving plate and repeat with remaining dough.

5. As soon as all of the churros are fried and coated, serve immediately with the dipping sauce.

Cider Doughnuts

DESCRIPTION *This lightly spiced buttermilk doughnut contains a good dose of apple cider. Do not use apple juice; only true apple cider will give you the depth of apple flavor you want. A classic cinnamon-sugar topping is fabulous. Cider Syrup Glaze (page 45) would work well, too.*

FIELD NOTES *An apple orchard in my town is famous for its cider doughnuts. I only recently found out that they are made from a mix that includes all sorts of preservatives and additives that we would never use at home. Undeterred, I set about creating an even tastier homemade version. Note that allspice is a spice unto itself and not a blend. These are quick to make and roll out very easily.*

LIFESPAN *These are best eaten as soon as possible.*

ⓒ ⏱

Yield: *about twenty-four 3-inch doughnuts*

INGREDIENTS

2½ cups all-purpose flour
1 cup sifted cake flour
2 teaspoons baking powder
2 teaspoons ground cinnamon
½ teaspoon baking soda
½ teaspoon salt
¼ teaspoon ground allspice
⅔ cup sugar

2 large eggs, at room temperature
1 cup apple cider, at room temperature
6 tablespoons (¾ stick) unsalted butter, melted and cooled
Flavorless vegetable oil for deep-frying, such as canola
1 recipe Cinnamon-Sugar Topping (optional; page 41)

DIRECTIONS

1. Whisk together both flours, the baking powder, cinnamon, baking soda, salt, and allspice in a medium-size bowl to aerate and combine.

2. In a large bowl, beat together the sugar and eggs with an electric mixer until pale and creamy, or whisk well by hand. Beat in the cider and melted butter until combined. Add the dry mixture in two batches and stir with a wooden spoon just until the dough comes together. Cover and refrigerate for at least 1 hour or up to overnight.

3. Line a rimmed baking sheet pan with a triple layer of paper towels. Heat 3 inches of oil in a deep pot or deep-fat fryer to 350° to 355°F.

4. While the oil is heating, dust the work surface with flour. Scrape the dough onto the surface, dust the top of the dough lightly with flour, and roll out to ½-inch thickness. Cut out doughnuts with a lightly floured 3-inch round cutter. Gently gather the scraps, press them together, roll out the dough, and cut out as many additional doughnuts as possible. Place the cinnamon sugar, if using, in a shallow bowl.

5. Fry a few doughnuts at a time; do not crowd. Fry until light golden brown, about 1 minute and 15 seconds, flip them over, and fry for about 1 minute and 15 seconds more, until light golden brown on the other side as well. Using a slotted spoon, remove each doughnut from the oil and drain thoroughly on paper towels.

6. If desired, immediately transfer the doughnuts to the bowl of cinnamon sugar and roll and toss them to coat completely. Repeat with the remaining dough.

Classic Doughnut Holes

DESCRIPTION *Most any doughnut recipe can be made into a doughnut hole, which is simply a spherical doughnut—typically a bit larger than the actual holes you see in ring-shaped doughnuts. I like them to be approximately 1½ inches across after frying. This recipe is a guide to turning any of the basic recipes in the book into this popular, snackable shape.*

FIELD NOTES *Size is the key; you want to make these ball-shaped doughnuts large enough so that you have a nice ratio of soft inside and crisp exterior. Any of the basic yeast-raised doughnuts will work, as will any of the basic fried cake-style recipes. For yeast-raised doughnuts, you need a round cutter that measures 1¼ inches across. For cake style, you need an ice cream scoop that measures about 1⁹⁄₁₆ inches across; I use a #40 Zeroll ice cream scoop, which makes perfectly round doughnut holes in the size I recommend. The amounts of toppings or glazes you ultimately need depend on the recipe you choose and how many different toppings or glazes you want to use. It is so easy to finish off your doughnut holes in more than one way that I highly recommend you try at least two different ways. Chocolate doughnut holes are so dark that it is hard to tell when they are done, so frying up a sample doughnut is a must.*

LIFESPAN *These are truly best eaten as soon as possible; small doughnuts get stale very quickly.*

$\mathcal{C}$

Yield: *depends on recipe chosen*

INGREDIENTS

1 recipe yeast-raised doughnuts, prepared through the first rise: Basic Yeast-Raised Doughnuts (page 28), Krispy Kreme Kopykat Doughnuts (page 32), or Chocolate Yeast-Raised Doughnuts (page 30); *or* 1 recipe cake-style dough: Old-Fashioned Buttermilk Doughnuts (page 22), Mashed Potato Doughnuts (page 23), Sour

Cream Doughnuts (page 24), or Chocolate Cake-Style Doughnuts (page 26)

Suggested glazes and toppings:
Soft and Sheer Sugar Glaze (page 35)
Cocoa Glaze (page 37)
Cinnamon-Sugar Topping (page 41)
Confectioners' sugar
Superfine sugar

DIRECTIONS

1. *For yeast-raised doughnuts:* Generously flour two rimmed baking sheet pans. Gently punch down the dough and divide it in half. Roll out one piece of dough on a lightly floured work surface to ⅓-inch thickness. (Doughnut holes are rolled slightly thinner than full-size doughnuts so they will puff up to the nice round shape that you want.) Cut out doughnut holes with a lightly floured 1¼-inch round cutter. Repeat with the remaining dough. Gently gather the scraps, press them together, roll out the dough, and cut out as many additional doughnut holes as possible. Place the holes, well spaced, on the prepared pans. Let rise in a warm, draft-free location until doubled in size, about 30 minutes.

2. Line a rimmed baking sheet pan with a triple layer of paper towels. Heat 3 inches of oil in a deep pot or deep-fat fryer to 350° to 355°F. When the oil is hot enough, fry a few holes at a time; do not crowd. Fry until light golden brown, about 1 minute, flip them over, and fry for about 1 minute more, until light golden brown on the other side as well. Using a slotted spoon, remove each hole from the oil and drain thoroughly on paper towels. Repeat with

the remaining holes. Cool until just barely warm to the touch.

3. *For cake-style doughnuts:* Line a rimmed baking sheet pan with a triple layer of paper towels. Heat 3 inches of oil in a deep pot or deep-fat fryer to 350° to 355°F. When the oil is hot enough, use a 1%₁₆-inch ice cream scoop to form round portions of the dough and drop (carefully) into the hot oil. Fry until light golden brown, about 1 minute, flip them over, and fry for about 1 minute more, until light golden brown on the other side as well. Using a slotted spoon, remove each hole from the oil and drain thoroughly on paper towels. Repeat with the remaining holes. Cool until just barely warm to the touch.

4. Line two rimmed baking sheet pans with cooling racks. If desired, toss the fried holes in the glaze(s) of your choice to coat all the way around, or simply dip just the tops. Let the glazed holes sit on the racks until the glaze sets, about 5 minutes.

5. If desired, alternatively, toss the holes one at a time in dry topping(s) of your choice to coat on all sides.

Coconut Cream–Filled Doughnuts with Coconut Glaze

DESCRIPTION *This yeast-raised doughnut is filled with coconut pastry cream and topped with a coconut glaze, both made with pure coconut milk for true coconut flavor.*

FIELD NOTES *I am not a fan of extracts other than vanilla and almond. I will resort to them occasionally, but I find many of the flavors to taste quite artificial. There is such a thing as coconut extract, but it cannot hold a candle to real coconut milk, which I have used in this recipe. Thankfully, coconut milk is now easy to find in larger supermarkets, often in the international aisle, or in smaller Asian markets. Make sure you get pure unsweetened coconut milk and not the highly sweetened cream of coconut that is used for piña coladas. When you open the can, if there is cream on top, stir it into the milk before measuring.*

LIFESPAN *These are best eaten as soon as possible but will keep at room temperature up to 2 hours.*

Yield: *about twenty-six 2½-inch filled doughnuts*

INGREDIENTS

Coconut pastry cream:
2 cups pure unsweetened coconut milk
2 large eggs
2 large egg yolks
½ cup granulated sugar
3 tablespoons cornstarch
Pinch of salt
I tablespoon unsalted butter, at room
  temperature
1½ teaspoons pure vanilla extract

I recipe Krispy Kreme Kopykat Doughnuts
  (page 32) or Basic Yeast-Raised
  Doughnuts (page 28), prepared through
  the first rise

Coconut glaze:
4 cups sifted confectioner' sugar
¾ cup pure unsweetened coconut milk
½ teaspoon pure vanilla extract
2 cups lightly packed sweetened long-shred
  coconut

Pastry bag and coupler fitted with a
  Bismarck #230 tip

DIRECTIONS

1. *For the pastry cream:* Bring the coconut milk to a boil in a medium-size nonreactive saucepan over medium heat; remove from the heat and cover to keep warm.

2. Meanwhile, whisk together the whole eggs, egg yolks, and granulated sugar in a medium-size bowl until creamy. Whisk in the cornstarch and salt until smooth.

3. Pour about one-quarter of the warm coconut milk into the egg mixture, whisking gently. Add the remaining milk and whisk to combine. Immediately pour the mixture back into the saucepan and cook over medium-low heat. Whisk almost continuously and watch for bubbles. As soon as the mixture begins to boil, whisk vigorously and constantly over the heat for 1 to 2 minutes. The pastry cream should be thick enough to mound when dropped from a spoon, but still be satiny. Remove from the heat and whisk in the butter and vanilla.

4. Let the pastry cream cool; stir occasionally to release the heat. When it is almost at room temperature, scrape it into an airtight container, press plastic wrap directly onto the surface (to keep a skin from forming), snap on the lid, and refrigerate until thoroughly chilled, at least 4 hours or up to 3 days.

5. *For the doughnuts:* Generously flour two rimmed baking sheet pans. Gently punch down the dough and divide it in half. Roll out one piece of dough on a lightly floured work surface to ½-inch thickness. Cut out doughnuts with a lightly floured 2½-inch round cutter. Repeat with the remaining dough. Gently gather the scraps, press them together, roll out the dough, and cut out as many additional doughnuts as possible.

6. Place the doughnuts, well spaced, on the prepared pans. Let rise in a warm, draft-free location until doubled in size, about 30 minutes.

7. Line two rimmed baking sheet pans with a triple layer of paper towels. Heat 3 inches of oil in a deep pot or deep-fat fryer to 350° to 355°F. When the oil is hot enough, fry a few doughnuts at a time; do not crowd. Fry until light golden brown, about 1½ minutes, flip them over, and fry for about 1½ minutes more, until light golden brown on the other side as well. Using a slotted spoon, remove each doughnut from the oil and drain thoroughly on paper towels. Repeat with the remaining doughnuts. Cool thoroughly.

8. Scrape the pastry cream into the pastry bag. Insert the tip into the side of a cooled doughnut. Squeeze the pastry bag and fill the doughnut with pastry cream just until the center of the doughnut slightly bulges. (You are aiming to pipe a generous 2 to 3 teaspoons of filling inside.) Repeat with the remaining doughnuts and pastry cream.

9. *For the glaze*: Place the confectioners' sugar in a medium bowl. Whisk in the coconut milk a little bit at a time until the desired consistency is reached. Whisk in the vanilla. Dip the top of each doughnut in the glaze. Sprinkle generously with shredded coconut while the glaze is still wet. Let sit for about 5 minutes to allow the glaze to set.

Crème Brûlée Doughnuts, Version #1

DESCRIPTION *These yeast-raised doughnuts are filled with rich pastry cream and the tops sprinkled with sugar and caramelized, just like crème brûlée.*

FIELD NOTES *Crème brûlée doughnuts are all the rage at certain popular doughnut shops, so I knew I had to include a recipe here. There are two versions in this book. This one is similar to the crème brûlée doughnuts that I have tasted in various doughnut emporiums. (Version #2, page 100, is my own original take on this concept.) Leftover pastry cream can be used to make individual trifles or dolloped on fruit. You need a propane torch or small kitchen torch for this recipe.*

LIFESPAN *These are best eaten as soon as possible but will keep at room temperature for up to 2 hours.*

Yield: *about twenty-six 2½-inch filled doughnuts*

INGREDIENTS

Crème brûlée pastry cream:
2 cups heavy cream
2 large eggs, at room temperature
½ cup sugar
2 tablespoons cornstarch
Pinch of salt
1 tablespoon unsalted butter
½ teaspoon pure vanilla extract

1 recipe Krispy Kreme Kopykat Doughnuts (page 32) or Basic Yeast-Raised Doughnuts (page 28), prepared through the first rise

Crème brûlée topping:
2 cups sugar

Pastry bag and coupler fitted with a Bismarck #230 tip

DIRECTIONS

1. *For the pastry cream:* Bring the cream to a boil in a medium-size nonreactive saucepan over medium heat; remove from the heat and cover to keep warm.

2. Meanwhile, whisk together the eggs and sugar in a medium-size bowl until creamy. Whisk in the cornstarch and salt until smooth. Pour about one-quarter of the warm cream into the egg mixture, whisking gently. Add the remaining cream and whisk to combine. Immediately pour the mixture back into the saucepan and cook over medium-low heat. Whisk almost continuously and watch for bubbles. As soon as the mixture begins to boil, whisk vigorously and constantly over the heat for 1 to 2 minutes. The pastry cream should be thick enough to mound when dropped from a spoon, but still be satiny. Remove from the heat and whisk in the butter and vanilla.

3. Let the pastry cream cool; stir occasionally to release the heat. When it is almost at room temperature, scrape it into an airtight container, press plastic wrap directly onto the surface (to keep

a skin from forming), snap on the lid, and refrigerate until thoroughly chilled, at least 4 hours and up to 2 days.

4. *For the doughnuts:* Generously flour two rimmed baking sheet pans. Gently punch down the dough and divide it in half. Roll out one piece of dough on a lightly floured work surface to ½-inch thickness. Cut out doughnuts with a lightly floured 2½-inch round cutter. Repeat with the remaining dough. Gently gather the scraps, press them together, roll out the dough, and cut out as many additional doughnuts as possible. Place the doughnuts, well spaced, on the prepared pans. Let rise in a warm, draft-free location until doubled in size, about 30 minutes.

5. Line two rimmed baking sheet pans with a triple layer of paper towels. Heat 3 inches of oil in a deep pot or deep-fat fryer to 350° to 355°F. When the oil is hot enough, fry a few doughnuts at a time; do not crowd. Fry until light golden brown, about 1½ minutes, flip them over, and fry for about 1½ minutes more, until light golden brown on the other side as well. Using

a slotted spoon, remove each doughnut from the oil and drain thoroughly on paper towels. Repeat with the remaining doughnuts. Cool thoroughly.

6. Scrape the pastry cream into the pastry bag. Insert the tip into the side of a cooled doughnut. Squeeze the pastry bag and fill the doughnut with pastry cream just until the center of the doughnut slightly bulges. (You are aiming to pipe a generous 2 to 3 teaspoons of filling inside.) Repeat with the remaining doughnuts and filling.

7. *For the crème brûlée topping*: Place the sugar in a shallow bowl. Line two rimmed baking sheet pans with aluminum foil. Dip the top of each doughnut in the sugar, gently pressing the doughnut into the sugar to encourage as much to adhere as possible. Place upright on the prepared pans. Use a teaspoon to sprinkle additional sugar on top of each doughnut. Use a propane torch to slowly and evenly melt the sugar so that it caramelizes on top of each doughnut. Alternatively, you can place the pans (one at a time) under a preheated broiler, set on high, and watch very carefully until the sugar melts and caramelizes. Let cool to harden the sugar. These must be "brûléed" right before serving.

Crème Brûlée Doughnuts, Version #2

 DESCRIPTION *Fried* pâte à choux *dough (from the basic French Cruller recipe) is filled with an extra rich, heavy cream-based pastry cream, and then dipped in caramelized sugar.*

 FIELD NOTES *The typical approach to crème brûlée doughnuts is featured in Version #1, but I couldn't resist trying to improve upon it. It occurred to me that using a tender, crisp* pâte à choux *for the outer casing would be more delicate and sophisticated. Also, the sugar crust created by the classic brûlée approach wasn't enough for me. Here the doughnuts are finished with a dip in hot caramelized sugar, similar to how you would make a classic French* croquembouche. *The caramelized sugar is very hot, so be careful. It is helpful to have a #40 Zeroll scoop for this recipe, which measures 1⁹⁄₁₆ inches across.*

 LIFESPAN *These are best eaten as soon as possible.*

Yield: *about twenty-two 2-inch filled doughnuts*

INGREDIENTS

1 recipe batter for French Crullers
(page 25)
1 recipe Crème Brûlée Pastry Cream
(page 98), chilled

Caramelized sugar topping:
1½ cups sugar
⅓ cup light corn syrup
⅓ cup water

Pastry bag and coupler fitted with a
Bismarck #230 tip

DIRECTIONS

1. Line two rimmed baking sheet pans with a triple layer of paper towels. Heat 3 inches of oil in a deep pot or deep-fat fryer to 350° to 355°F. When the oil is hot enough, use a 1⁹⁄₁₆-inch ice cream scoop to form round portions of dough and drop (carefully) into the hot oil. Fry a few at a time; do not crowd. Fry until light golden brown, about 2½ minutes, flip them over, and fry about 2½ minutes more, until light golden brown on the other side as well. Using a slotted spoon, remove each doughnut from the oil and drain thoroughly on paper towels. Repeat with the remaining dough. Cool thoroughly.

2. Scrape the cold pastry cream into the pastry bag. Insert the tip into the side of a cooled doughnut. Squeeze the pastry bag and fill the doughnut with pastry cream just until the center of the doughnut slightly bulges. (You are aiming to pipe about 1½ to 2 teaspoons of filling inside.) Repeat with the remaining doughnuts and pastry cream.

3. *For the caramelized sugar topping*: Line two rimmed baking sheet pans with aluminum foil and lightly coat the foil with nonstick cooking spray. Place the sugar, corn syrup, and water in a heavy-duty medium-size saucepan and stir to combine. Bring to a boil over medium-high heat, swirling the pan once or twice. Continue to boil the mixture until it reaches a deep golden color. Immediately plunge the bottom of the pot into a baking dish or sink filled with ice water until any sputtering and/or boiling ceases. (This stops the cooking so that the caramel won't get too dark.)

4. Immediately place the pot on the work surface next to the racks of filled doughnuts. Very carefully, pick up a doughnut and dip the top in the caramelized sugar. Take care not to get any of the melted (and still very hot) sugar on your fingers. Place the doughnut upright on the prepared sheet pan to cool; repeat with the remaining doughnuts. (There will be caramelized sugar left over; it's just easier to use a generous quantity.) Let the caramelized sugar topping harden, about 10 minutes, though the time can vary with the humidity.

Double-Chocolate Ganache Doughnuts

DESCRIPTION *This rich chocolate-cake doughnut is slathered with chocolate ganache and an optional sprinkling of chocolate jimmies and/or chocolate shavings—in which case you can call them Triple-Chocolate!*

FIELD NOTES *Chocolate, chocolate, and more chocolate. Many doughnut shop chocolate doughnuts, in my opinion, lack deep chocolate color and flavor. This recipe knocks that issue out of the park with a chocolate-packed experience. I like to leave some with just ganache on top, sprinkle some with jimmies, and top others with chocolate shavings for a three-in-one treat. You will have extra ganache left over. It keeps for up to 1 month in the freezer and can be melted for a quick ice cream topping. To make the chocolate shavings, use a large chef's knife or a vegetable peeler to shave off shards and curls from a block of semisweet or bittersweet chocolate.*

LIFESPAN *These are best eaten as soon as possible.*

Yield: *about fourteen 3-inch doughnuts*

INGREDIENTS

1 recipe Chocolate Cake-Style Doughnuts
(page 26), cut into 3-inch rings, fried, and
beginning to cool

1 recipe Dark Chocolate Ganache Glaze
(page 39)

Chocolate jimmies/sprinkles (optional)
Chocolate shavings (optional)

DIRECTIONS

Dip the top of each doughnut into the
glaze or spread it using a small offset
spatula. If you like, sprinkle jimmies
and chocolate shavings on top of some
of the doughnuts while the glaze is cool
but still wet. Let sit for about 5 minutes to allow the glaze to set.

Double-Espresso Doughnuts

DESCRIPTION *These cake-style doughnuts have a deep, dark espresso flavor thanks to the inclusion of instant espresso powder. If you love coffee, give these a try—otherwise, steer clear! They are potent.*

FIELD NOTES *Instant espresso powder has a finer texture and a more powerful flavor than regular instant coffee. You need this specialty product to get the intended result. Look for Medaglia d'Oro instant espresso powder in supermarkets, or you can order it from King Arthur Flour (see Resources, page 173). The instant espresso is used in the glaze as well. If you want the coffee flavor to be even more pronounced, increase the amount of espresso powder in the glaze—just taste it as you are preparing it and add more if desired.*

LIFESPAN *These are best eaten as soon as possible.*

Yield: *about twelve 3-inch doughnuts*

INGREDIENTS

1 recipe Sour Cream Doughnuts (page 24), prepared substituting 2 tablespoons instant espresso powder for the nutmeg, cut into 3-inch rings, fried, and beginning to cool

1 recipe Soft and Sheer Sugar Glaze (page 35), prepared whisking 1 tablespoon instant espresso powder with the water

DIRECTIONS

Dip the top of each doughnut into the glaze and let sit for about 5 minutes to allow the glaze to set.

Double-Lemon Glazed Doughnuts

 **DESCRIPTION** *Lemon zest is added to the batter and glaze of these old-fashioned cake-style doughnuts.*

 **FIELD NOTES** *I use a Microplane zester to create very finely textured lemon zest. The texture incorporates easily into the doughnut batter and doesn't interfere with the glaze. If you grate your zest using a different kind of tool, the measurements will not be the same.*

 **LIFESPAN** *These are best eaten as soon as possible.*

Yield: *sixteen to eighteen 3-inch doughnuts, depending on recipe chosen*

INGREDIENTS

1 tablespoon finely minced lemon zest

2 recipes Citrus Glaze, made with freshly squeezed lemon juice (page 35)

1 recipe Old-Fashioned Buttermilk Doughnuts (page 22) or Mashed Potato Doughnuts (page 23), prepared with 1 tablespoon finely minced lemon zest added to the batter, cut into 3-inch rings, fried, and beginning to cool

DIRECTIONS

1. Line two rimmed baking sheet pans with aluminum foil or parchment paper.

2. Whisk the lemon zest into the freshly prepared glaze. Dip the top of each doughnut into the glaze or spread it using a small offset spatula. Let the doughnuts sit on the prepared pans until the glaze sets, about 5 minutes.

Doughnut Shop
Glazed Doughnuts

🔘 **DESCRIPTION** *Just like what you would find at the local doughnut shop—this soft, yeast-raised, ring-shaped doughnut has a creamy, slightly opaque, slightly sticky, sugary glaze.*

🔘 **FIELD NOTES** *This is my take on a Krispy Kreme glazed doughnut. The glaze has butter in it, which gives it a thicker, creamier appearance and flavor than the basic sugar glaze. Feel free to try this glaze on other doughnuts, too.*

🔘 **LIFESPAN** *These are best eaten as soon as possible, although they will still be soft and springy the next day if stored in an airtight container at room temperature.*

C

Yield: *twenty-two 3-inch ring-shaped doughnuts*

INGREDIENTS

Glaze:
9 tablespoons unsalted butter
3 cups sifted confectioners' sugar
6 to 9 tablespoons hot water
2¼ teaspoons pure vanilla extract

1 recipe Krispy Kreme Kopykat Doughnuts (page 32), cut into 3-inch rings, fried, and beginning to cool

DIRECTIONS

1. *For the glaze*: Melt the butter in a medium-size saucepan. Off the heat, whisk in the confectioners' sugar, a bit at a time, making sure it incorporates smoothly, with no lumps. Whisk in the water slowly, adding only enough to reach the desired consistency. It should be slightly thick and opaque, but still fluid. Whisk in the vanilla.

2. Dip the top of each doughnut in the glaze and let sit for about 5 minutes to allow the glaze to set.

French Crullers with Grand Marnier Glaze

 **DESCRIPTION** *These light, airy, and crisp French crullers have deep ridges created from the piping tip—all the better to hold the orange Grand Marnier glaze. The addition of orange flower water is optional, but adds a delicacy that matches the doughnut's texture.*

 **FIELD NOTES** *Orange flower water can be found in specialty stores or some supermarket international aisles. You could use a different large star tip, but the Ateco #847 makes beautiful deep ridges and is the one I prefer.*

 **LIFESPAN** *These are best eaten as soon as possible.*

Yield: *about nine 3-inch crullers*

INGREDIENTS

Grand Marnier glaze:
1 cup sifted confectioners' sugar
2 tablespoons milk
1 teaspoon Grand Marnier
½ teaspoon orange flower water (optional)

1 recipe French Crullers (page 25), fried and beginning to cool

DIRECTIONS

Whisk together the glaze ingredients in a small bowl until smooth. Immediately apply the glaze all over the tops of the crullers with a pastry brush or, alternatively, dip the tops of the crullers into the glaze. Let sit for 5 minutes to allow the glaze to set.

German Chocolate Cake Doughnuts

DESCRIPTION *A basic chocolate cake doughnut is smeared with a thick topping of classic German chocolate cake frosting, which features coconut and pecans.*

FIELD NOTES *This topping is cooked on top of the stove and comes together very easily. Make sure to use evaporated milk and not sweetened condensed milk; they will be side by side on the supermarket shelf. The topping can be made a few days ahead, so take advantage of this time saver.*

LIFESPAN *These are best eaten as soon as possible.*

Yield: *about fourteen 3-inch doughnuts*

INGREDIENTS

Topping:
Scant 1 cup evaporated milk
Scant 1 cup sugar
3 large egg yolks
7½ tablespoons unsalted butter, at room
temperature, cut into pieces
1 teaspoon pure vanilla extract

1½ cups sweetened long-shred coconut
Scant 1 cup pecan halves, toasted (page 10)
and chopped

1 recipe Chocolate Cake-Style Doughnuts
(page 26), cut into 3-inch rings, baked,
and beginning to cool

DIRECTIONS

1. *For the topping:* Place the evaporated milk and sugar in a large saucepan and whisk to combine. Whisk in the egg yolks and butter. Gently cook over medium heat until the mixture reaches a simmer; continue to cook, whisking frequently, until it thickens and slightly darkens, about 5 minutes. Remove from the heat and stir in the coconut and pecans. Cool to room temperature, stirring occasionally to release the heat.

The topping may be stored for up to 3 days in an airtight container in the refrigerator. Bring to room temperature before using.

2. While the doughnuts are still slightly warm, use a small offset spatula to spread the topping all over the tops.

Gingerbread Doughnuts with Lemon Glaze

DESCRIPTION *These cake-style doughnuts have a medium-dark color and the flavor of gingerbread.*

FIELD NOTES *Use dark brown sugar to boost the rich molasses flavor. Also, make sure your spices are fresh in order to highlight this doughnut's spicy flavor profile.*

LIFESPAN *These are best eaten as soon as possible.*

Yield: *about twelve 3-inch doughnuts*

INGREDIENTS

1¾ cups all-purpose flour
1¼ cups sifted cake flour
1 tablespoon plus 1 teaspoon ground
cinnamon
1 tablespoon ground ginger
1 tablespoon baking powder
½ teaspoon baking soda
½ teaspoon salt
½ teaspoon ground allspice
¼ teaspoon white pepper

2 large eggs, at room temperature
2 large egg yolks, at room temperature
⅔ cup firmly packed dark brown sugar
⅔ cup full-fat sour cream, at room
temperature
6 tablespoons unsulfured molasses
¼ cup flavorless vegetable oil, such as
canola, plus more for deep-frying
1 recipe Citrus Glaze (page 35), made with
freshly squeezed lemon juice

DIRECTIONS

1. Whisk together both flours, the cinnamon, ginger, baking powder, baking soda, salt, allspice, and white pepper in a medium-size bowl to aerate and combine.

2. In a large bowl, beat together the whole eggs, egg yolks, and brown sugar with an electric mixer until pale and creamy, or whisk well by hand. Beat in the sour cream, molasses, and oil until combined. Add the dry mixture in two batches and stir with a wooden spoon just until the dough comes together. Cover and refrigerate for at least 2 hours or up to overnight.

3. Remove the dough from the refrigerator. Line a rimmed baking sheet pan with a triple layer of paper towels. Heat 3 inches of oil in a deep pot or deep-fat fryer to 350° to 355°F.

4. While the oil is heating, dust the work surface generously with flour. Scrape the dough (it will be soft) onto the sur-

face, dust the top of the dough lightly with flour, and roll out to ½-inch thickness. Cut out doughnuts with a lightly floured 3-inch round cutter. Gently gather the scraps, press them together, roll out the dough, and cut out as many additional doughnuts as possible.

5. Fry a few doughnuts at a time; do not crowd. Fry until light golden brown, about 1½ minutes, flip them over, and fry for about 1½ minutes more, until light golden brown on the other side as well. Using a slotted spoon, remove each doughnut from the oil and drain thoroughly on paper towels. Repeat with the remaining dough.

6. While the doughnuts are still slightly warm, dip the tops into the glaze or spread it using a small offset spatula. Let sit about 5 minutes to allow the glaze to set.

Grape Expectations

⬭ **DESCRIPTION** *Yeast-raised doughnuts are filled with grape jelly and covered with a dusting of instant grape beverage powder. Yes, you read that right.*

⬭ **FIELD NOTES** *This is another homage to a Voodoo Doughnut (voodoodonut.com) classic. They call theirs Grape Ape and it is slightly different, but my adaptation is a great home version. These are sweet and very fruity. Feel free to use other flavors of jam or jelly with coordinating (or contrasting) powdered beverage toppings. If you have grape juice around, use it for the glaze; otherwise water will work just fine.*

⬭ **LIFESPAN** *These are best eaten as soon as possible.*

Yield: *about twenty-eight 2½-inch filled doughnuts*

INGREDIENTS

1¼ cups grape jelly or jam
1 recipe Krispy Kreme Kopykat Doughnuts (page 32) or Basic Yeast-Raised Doughnuts (page 28), cut into 2½-inch rounds, fried, and beginning to cool

2 recipes Soft and Sheer Sugar Glaze (page 35), substituting Welch's grape juice for the water
Powdered grape beverage powder, such as Kool-Aid

Pastry bag and coupler fitted with a Bismarck #230 tip

DIRECTIONS

1. Scrape the jelly into the pastry bag. Insert the tip into the side of a doughnut. Squeeze the pastry bag and fill the doughnut with jelly just until the center of the doughnut slightly bulges. (You are aiming to pipe a generous 2 to 3 teaspoons of filling inside.) Repeat with the remaining doughnuts and jelly.

2. Dip the top of each doughnut into the glaze or spread it using a small offset spatula; you want a very sheer layer, just enough to help the powdered beverage stick. Generously sprinkle the powdered juice drink on top while the glaze is still wet. Let sit for about 5 minutes to allow the glaze to set.

Honey Cream–Filled Doughnuts with Milk and Honey Glaze

DESCRIPTION *This yeast-raised doughnut is filled with honey-sweetened pastry cream and topped with a milk and honey glaze.*

FIELD NOTES *I have suggested starting with one of the "regular" yeast-raised doughnut recipes, but you can use this filling and glaze with Chocolate Yeast-Raised Doughnuts (page 30) as well. Your choice of honey will determine the flavor of the glaze. In general, the lighter the honey color, the lighter the honey taste. I like using orange blossom, acacia, or clover honey.*

LIFESPAN *These are best eaten as soon as possible but will keep at room temperature for up to 2 hours.*

Yield: *about twenty-six 2½-inch filled doughnuts*

INGREDIENTS

Honey pastry cream:
2 cups whole milk
2 large eggs
2 large egg yolks
¼ cup honey
¼ cup cornstarch
Pinch of salt
¼ cup (½ stick) unsalted butter, at room
    temperature, cut into pieces
½ teaspoon pure vanilla extract

1 recipe Krispy Kreme Kopykat Doughnuts
    (page 32) or Basic Yeast-Raised
    Doughnuts (page 28), prepared through
    the first rise

Milk and honey glaze:
¾ cup whole milk
6 tablespoons honey
4½ cups sifted confectioners' sugar

Pastry bag and coupler fitted with a
    Bismarck #230 tip

DIRECTIONS

1. *For the pastry cream*: Bring the milk to a boil in a medium-size nonreactive saucepan over medium heat; remove from the heat and cover to keep warm.

2. Meanwhile, whisk together the whole eggs, egg yolks, and honey in a medium-size bowl until creamy. Whisk in the cornstarch and salt until smooth. Pour about one-quarter of the warm milk into the egg mixture, whisking gently. Add the remaining milk and whisk to combine. Immediately pour the mixture back into the saucepan and cook over medium-low heat. Whisk almost continuously and watch for bubbles. As soon as the mixture begins to boil, whisk vigorously and constantly over the heat for 1 to 2 minutes. The pastry cream should be thick enough to mound when dropped from a spoon, but still be satiny. Remove from the heat and whisk in the butter and vanilla.

3. Let the pastry cream cool; stir occasionally to release the heat. When the pastry cream is almost at room temperature, scrape it into an airtight container, press plastic wrap directly onto the surface (to keep a skin from forming), snap on the lid, and refrigerate until thoroughly chilled, at least 4 hours and up to 2 days.

4. *For the doughnuts*: Generously flour two rimmed baking sheet pans. Gently punch down the dough and divide it in half. Roll out one piece of dough on a lightly floured work surface to ½-inch thickness. Cut out doughnuts with a lightly floured 2½-inch round cutter. Repeat with the remaining dough. Gently gather the scraps, press them together, roll out the dough, and cut out as many additional doughnuts as possible. Place the doughnuts, well spaced, on the prepared pans. Let rise in a warm, draft-free location until doubled in size, about 30 minutes.

5. Line two rimmed baking sheet pans with a triple layer of paper towels. Heat 3 inches of oil in a deep pot or deep-fat fryer to 350° to 355°F. When the oil is hot enough, fry a few doughnuts at

a time; do not crowd. Fry until light golden brown, about 1½ minutes, flip them over, and fry for about 1½ minutes more, until light golden brown on the other side as well. Using a slotted spoon, remove each doughnut from the oil and drain thoroughly on paper towels. Repeat with the remaining doughnuts. Cool thoroughly.

6. Scrape the pastry cream into the pastry bag. Insert the tip into the side of a cooled doughnut. Squeeze the pastry bag and fill the doughnut with pastry cream just until the center of the doughnut slightly bulges. (You are aiming to pipe a generous 2 to 3 teaspoons of filling inside.) Repeat with the remaining doughnuts and pastry cream.

7. *For the glaze*: Place the milk and honey in a small saucepan and heat over low heat just until warm, stirring to dissolve the honey. Remove from the heat. Place the confectioners' sugar in a medium-size bowl and whisk in the warm honey mixture until smooth.

8. Dip the top of each doughnut in the glaze and let sit for about 5 minutes to allow the glaze to set.

Lemon Meringue Doughnuts

DESCRIPTION *For lemon lovers, this yeast-raised doughnut is filled with puckery lemon curd, topped with a swirl of meringue, and browned with a propane torch. Gorgeous and impressive.*

FIELD NOTES *Yes, I said propane torch. You could brown these under the broiler, keeping a close eye on them, but it is so much easier to use a mini kitchen propane torch, which will come in handy when making the two versions of crème brûlée doughnuts (pages 97–100). Lemon curd can be found in jars in some supermarkets and specialty shops, but it is never as tangy as homemade; it is worth the time and effort to make your own. And as long as you are making it, you might as well take the time to squeeze your own lemon juice, too. The meringue would be difficult to make in double the amount, so I have recommended you make a half batch of the doughnuts.*

LIFESPAN *These are best eaten as soon as possible.*

Yield: *about thirteen 2½-inch doughnuts*

INGREDIENTS

Lemon curd:
- ¼ cup freshly squeezed lemon juice
- 2 large eggs
- 1 large egg yolk
- ¾ cup sugar
- 6 tablespoons (¾ stick) unsalted butter, at room temperature, cut into pieces
- ½ teaspoon finely grated lemon zest (optional)

Half a recipe Krispy Kreme Kopykat Doughnuts (page 32) or Basic Yeast-Raised Doughnuts (page 28), prepared through the first rise

Meringue:
- 4 large egg whites
- 1 cup sugar
- Heaping ¼ teaspoon cream of tartar

Pastry bag and coupler fitted with a Bismarck #230 tip
Pastry bag and coupler fitted with a large star tip, such as Ateco #847

DIRECTIONS

1. *For the lemon curd:* Place the lemon juice, whole eggs, egg yolk, and sugar in the top of a double boiler. Whisk to break up the eggs. Add the butter. Fill the bottom of the double boiler with enough hot water to just reach the bottom of the top pan; place the top pan over the bottom pan. Place the double boiler over medium heat and bring the water to a simmer.

2. Whisk the mixture frequently over the simmering water until it reaches 180°F on a thermometer. (The temperature is more important than the time it takes; the mixture should not simmer.) The curd will thicken and form a soft shape when dropped by a spoon. If desired, stir in the lemon zest after removing from the heat. Cool the curd to room temperature, scrape it into an airtight container, place a piece of plastic wrap directly onto the surface (to keep a skin from forming), and refrigerate until chilled, at least 4 hours or up to 1 week.

3. Generously flour a rimmed baking sheet pan. Gently punch down the dough and divide it in half. Roll out one piece of dough on a lightly floured work surface to ½-inch thickness. Cut out doughnuts with a lightly floured 2½-inch round cutter. Repeat with the remaining dough. Gently gather the scraps, press them together, roll out the dough, and cut out as many additional doughnuts as possible. Place the doughnuts, well spaced, on the prepared pan. Let rise in a warm, draft-free location until doubled in size, about 30 minutes.

4. Line a rimmed baking sheet pan with a triple layer of paper towels. Heat 3 inches of oil in a deep pot or deep-fat fryer to 350° to 355°F. When the oil is hot enough, fry a few doughnuts at a time; do not crowd. Fry until light

golden brown, about 1½ minutes, flip them over, and fry for about 1½ minutes more, until light golden brown on the other side as well. Using a slotted spoon, remove each doughnut from the oil and drain thoroughly on paper towels. Repeat with the remaining doughnuts. Cool thoroughly.

5. Scrape the lemon curd into a pastry bag fitted with a coupler and a #230 tip. Insert the tip into the top of doughnut. Squeeze the pastry bag and fill the doughnut with lemon curd just until the center of the doughnut slightly bulges. (You are aiming to pipe a generous 2 to 3 teaspoons of filling inside.) Repeat with the remaining doughnuts and lemon curd.

6. *For the meringue*: Whisk together the egg whites and sugar in the top of a double boiler. Fill the bottom of the double boiler with enough hot water to just reach the bottom of the top pan; place the top pan over the bottom pan. Place the double boiler over medium heat and bring the water to a boil, whisking the egg whites occasionally. As the temperature nears 140°F, whisk frequently. When the temperature reaches 160°F, remove the pan from the heat, add the cream of tartar, and beat on high speed with a handheld electric mixer right in the pot until a thick meringue forms. (Alternatively, you can transfer the mixture to a stand mixer and beat with the balloon whip attachment). Keep beating the meringue until it cools to a barely warm temperature, about 5 minutes.

7. Immediately scrape the meringue into a clean pastry bag fitted with a large star tip. Pipe a generous swirl of meringue on top of each doughnut, covering the hole where you inserted the lemon curd. Brown the meringue with a mini propane torch.

Jelly Doughnuts

DESCRIPTION *Yeast-raised doughnuts filled with jelly or jam are a classic, and I present you with some options about how to fill them—either before or after frying. I also offer a choice of a roll in superfine, granulated, or confectioners' sugar to finish them off.*

FIELD NOTES *I have a beef with jelly doughnuts. I think the best ones are filled with really fruity, chunky jams. The problem with this is that you cannot pipe these through a pastry bag into the doughnut after baking, so if you want to use a jam or preserve with this texture, you have to fill the doughnuts before frying. If you like a smooth jelly, then you have your choice of technique and can fill them before or after.*

LIFESPAN *These are best eaten as soon as possible, although they will still be soft and springy the next day if stored in an airtight container at room temperature.*

C

Yield: *about twenty-six 2½-inch filled doughnuts*

INGREDIENTS

1 recipe Krispy Kreme Kopykat Doughnuts (page 32) or Basic Yeast-Raised Doughnuts (page 28), prepared through the first rise

1¼ cups jam, fruit preserve, or jelly of your choice

Superfine, granulated, or confectioners' sugar

Pastry bag and coupler fitted with a Bismarck #230 tip

DIRECTIONS

1. Generously flour two rimmed baking sheet pans. Gently punch down the dough and divide it in half.

2. *If using a chunky jam or fruit preserve*: Roll out one piece of dough on a lightly floured work surface to ¼-inch thickness. Cut out dough rounds with a lightly floured 2½-inch round cutter. Repeat with the remaining dough. Gently gather the scraps, press them together, roll out the dough, and cut out as many additional rounds as possible. Make sure you end up with an even number. Using two cereal spoons, dollop about 2 teaspoons of jam in the centers of half of the dough rounds. Dip a pastry brush in room-temperature water and lightly brush the edges of the dough around the jam. Place a plain round on top of each filled round and press the edges together with your fingertips to seal them well.

3. *If using a smooth jelly:* Roll out one piece of dough on a lightly floured work surface to ½-inch thickness. Cut out doughnuts with a lightly floured 2½-inch round cutter. Repeat with the remaining dough. Gently gather the scraps, press them together, roll out the dough, and cut out as many additional doughnuts as possible.

4. Place the doughnuts, well spaced, on the prepared pans. Let rise in a warm,

draft-free location until doubled in size, about 30 minutes

5. Line two rimmed baking sheet pans with a triple layer of paper towels. Heat 3 inches of oil in a deep pot or deep-fat fryer to 350° to 355°F. When the oil is hot enough, fry a few doughnuts at a time; do not crowd. Fry until light golden brown, about 1½ minutes, flip them over, and fry for about 1½ minutes more, until light golden brown on the other side as well. Using a slotted spoon, remove each doughnut from the oil and drain thoroughly on paper towels. Repeat with the remaining doughnuts.

6. *For chunky jam–filled doughnuts*: While the doughnuts are still warm, toss them in the sugar of your choice to cover completely.

7. *For smooth jelly–filled doughnuts*: While the doughnuts are still warm, roll them on all sides in the sugar of your choice to cover completely. Let the doughnuts cool. Scrape the jelly into the pastry bag. Insert the tip into the side of a doughnut. Squeeze the pastry bag and fill the doughnut with jelly just until the center of the doughnut slightly bulges. (You are aiming to pipe a generous 2 to 3 teaspoons of filling inside.) Repeat with the remaining doughnuts.

Maple-Bacon Doughnuts

DESCRIPTION *This log-shaped yeast-raised doughnut is topped with a maple syrup glaze and bits of crispy bacon.*

FIELD NOTES *Bacon has been making the rounds in the bakery kitchen as of late and it has a natural affinity for maple flavor, here provided by pure maple syrup incorporated into a confectioners' sugar glaze. Try to find Grade B syrup—it is darker and has a more pronounced maple flavor. (Did you know that most of the pricier maple syrups are Grade A, which is actually lighter in color and flavor?) Read the labels and be sure not to use a corn syrup–based pancake syrup. Cook the bacon any way you prefer; just make sure it's crisp. Need I mention that this is the perfect breakfast or brunch doughnut?*

LIFESPAN *These are best eaten as soon as possible.*

☺ 🎀

Yield: *about thirty 4-inch log-shaped doughnuts*

INGREDIENTS

1 recipe Krispy Kreme Kopykat Doughnuts (page 32) or Basic Yeast-Raised Doughnuts (page 28), prepared through the first rise

Maple glaze:
¾ cup pure maple syrup
3 cups sifted confectioners' sugar

24 slices bacon, cooked until crisp and cut or broken into ½-inch pieces

DIRECTIONS

1. Generously flour two rimmed baking sheet pans. Gently punch down the dough and divide it in half. Roll out one piece of dough on a lightly floured work surface into a rectangle ½ inch thick. Use a pizza wheel to cut the dough into 4 x 1½-inch strips. Repeat with the remaining dough. Place the strips, well spaced, on the prepared pans. Let rise in a warm, draft-free location until doubled in size, about 30 minutes.

2. Line two rimmed baking sheet pans with a triple layer of paper towels. Heat 3 inches of oil in a deep pot or deep-fat fryer to 350° to 355°F. When the oil is hot enough, fry a few logs at a time; do not crowd. Fry until light golden brown, about 1 minute and 20 seconds, flip them over, and fry for about 1 minute and 20 seconds more, until light golden brown on the other side as well. Using a slotted spoon, remove each log from the oil and drain thoroughly on paper towels. Repeat with the remaining logs. Cool until just barely warm to the touch.

3. *For the glaze*: Heat the maple syrup in a medium-size saucepan set over medium-low heat just until it is warm, 2 to 3 minutes. Remove from the heat and whisk in the confectioners' sugar until completely smooth. Dip the top of each log in the glaze or spread it with a small offset spatula. Scatter crisp bacon pieces on top and let sit for about 5 minutes to allow the glaze to set.

Marshmallow Fluff and Peanut Butter Doughnuts

 **DESCRIPTION** *This is just like a Fluffernutter sandwich—that fave childhood combo of marshmallow creme and peanut butter—but this time in the form of a yeast-raised doughnut. The marshmallow is tucked inside the doughnut and the top is coated in a crunchy peanut butter glaze.*

 **FIELD NOTES** *Lightly spritz your teaspoons with nonstick cooking spray to make dolloping the marshmallow creme easier.*

 **LIFESPAN** *These are best eaten as soon as possible.*

Yield: *about twenty-six 2½-inch filled doughnuts*

INGREDIENTS

1 recipe Krispy Kreme Kopykat Doughnuts (page 32) or Basic Yeast-Raised Doughnuts (page 28), prepared through the first rise

1 cup plus 2 tablespoons marshmallow creme, such as Fluff

1 recipe Peanut Butter Glaze (page 40)

DIRECTIONS

1. Generously flour two rimmed baking sheet pans. Gently punch down the dough and divide it in half. Roll out one piece of dough on a lightly floured work surface to ¼-inch thickness. Cut out dough rounds with a lightly floured 2½-inch round cutter. Repeat with the remaining dough. Gently gather the scraps, press them together, roll out the dough, and cut out as many additional rounds as possible. Make sure you end up with an even number.

2. Using two cereal spoons, dollop about 2 teaspoons of marshmallow creme in the centers of half of the dough rounds. Dip a pastry brush in room-temperature water and lightly brush the edges of the dough around the marshmallow filling. Place a plain round on top of each filled round and press the edges together with your fingertips to seal them well.

3. Place the doughnuts, well spaced, on the prepared pans. Let rise in a warm, draft-free location until doubled in size, about 30 minutes.

4. Line two rimmed baking sheet pans with a triple layer of paper towels. Heat 3 inches of oil in a deep pot or deep-fat fryer to 350° to 355°F. When the oil is hot enough, fry a few doughnuts at a time; do not crowd. Fry until light golden brown, about 1½ minutes, flip them over, and fry for about 1½ minutes more, until light golden brown on the other side as well. Using a slotted spoon, remove each doughnut from the oil and drain thoroughly on paper towels. Repeat with the remaining doughnuts.

5. While the doughnuts are still slightly warm, dip the tops into the glaze or spread it using a small offset spatula. Let sit for about 5 minutes to allow the glaze to set.

Nutella Doughnuts with Gianduja Ganache

 **DESCRIPTION** *These yeast-raised doughnuts are filled with Nutella, the delicious chocolate-hazelnut spread, and topped with a gianduja ganache. Gianduja is a hazelnut chocolate, in this case milk chocolate that is melted with cream to make a gianduja glaze. This is one decadent doughnut!*

 **FIELD NOTES** *You will most likely have to go to a specialty store or mail-order the gianduja. I use Callebaut, which can be found at chocosphere.com (see Resources, page 173). Nutella can usually be found next to the peanut butter at the supermarket.*

 **LIFESPAN** *These are best eaten as soon as possible, although they will still be soft and springy the next day if stored in an airtight container at room temperature.*

Yield: *about twenty-six 2½-inch doughnuts*

INGREDIENTS

1 recipe Krispy Kreme Kopykat Doughnuts
(page 32) or Basic Yeast-Raised
Doughnuts (page 28), prepared through
the first rise
1¼ cups Nutella

Gianduja ganache:
¾ cup plus 2 tablespoons heavy cream
14 ounces milk chocolate gianduja, such as
Callebaut, finely chopped

DIRECTIONS

1. Generously flour two rimmed baking
sheet pans. Gently punch down the
dough and divide it in half. Roll out
one piece of dough on a lightly floured
work surface to ¼-inch thickness. Cut
out dough rounds with a lightly floured
2½-inch round cutter. Repeat with the
remaining dough. Gently gather the
scraps, press them together, roll out the
dough, and cut out as many additional
rounds as possible. Make sure you end
up with an even number.

2. Using two cereal spoons, dollop about
2 teaspoons of Nutella in the centers of
half of the dough rounds. Dip a pastry
brush in room-temperature water and
lightly brush the edges of the dough
around the Nutella filling. Place a plain
round on top of each filled round and
press the edges together with your fingertips to seal them well.

3. Place the doughnuts, well spaced, on
the prepared pans. Let rise in a warm,
draft-free location until doubled in size,
about 30 minutes.

4. While the doughnuts are rising, make
the ganache: Bring the cream to a boil
in a large saucepan over medium heat.
Remove from the heat and immediately

sprinkle the gianduja into the cream.
Cover and let sit for 5 minutes. Gently
stir the ganache until smooth—the heat
of the cream should melt the gianduja.
If the gianduja does not melt completely, place the pan over very low
heat and stir the ganache often, until
melted, taking care not to burn it. Cool
until warm but still fluid.

5. While the ganache is cooling, line 2
rimmed baking sheet pans with a triple
layer of paper towels. Heat 3 inches
of oil in a deep pot or deep-fat fryer
to 350° to 355°F. When the oil is hot
enough, fry a few doughnuts at a time;
do not crowd. Fry until light golden
brown, about 1½ minutes, flip them
over, and fry for about 1½ minutes
more, until light golden brown on
the other side as well. Using a slotted
spoon, remove each doughnut from
the oil and drain thoroughly on paper
towels. Repeat with the remaining
doughnuts.

6. While the doughnuts are still slightly
warm, dip the tops in the ganache. Let
sit for about 5 minutes to allow the
ganache to set.

Old-Fashioned Lard-Fried Doughnuts

DESCRIPTION *These moist, old-fashioned doughnuts are flavored with mace, which is the outer coating of the nutmeg and has a similar flavor. Toss half in cinnamon sugar and half in confectioners' sugar.*

FIELD NOTES *My very good friend Jeff Rys is the second generation in his family to make these doughnuts, and they are busy handing it down to the third. He believes it originally came from an old 1950s cookbook, but his family and I have adapted it. It is traditional in their family to make these with the kids, who love to shake them in paper bags with the toppings, which works only if you are making very small doughnuts or holes. These are larger doughnuts, though, and I prefer to coat them one at a time in the dry toppings. Lard can be found in most supermarkets near the butter. As a frying medium, it lends a very distinctive flavor that you will either love or not. This dough is rolled immediately and does not need refrigeration to firm up.*

LIFESPAN *These are best eaten as soon as possible.*

© ☺ ☺

Yield: *about twenty 3-inch doughnuts*

INGREDIENTS

4 cups all-purpose flour
4 teaspoons baking powder
1 teaspoon ground mace
1 teaspoon freshly grated nutmeg
½ teaspoon salt
1 cup granulated sugar
2 large eggs, at room temperature,
  separated

1 cup whole milk, at room temperature
½ cup vegetable shortening, melted and
  slightly cooled
Lard for deep-frying
Half a recipe Cinnamon-Sugar Topping
  (page 41)
Confectioners' sugar

DIRECTIONS

1. Whisk together the flour, baking powder, mace, nutmeg, and salt in a medium-size bowl to aerate and combine.

2. In a large bowl, beat together the granulated sugar and egg yolks with an electric mixer until combined, or whisk well by hand. Beat in the milk and the dry mixture alternately in two batches with a wooden spoon and stir just until the dough comes together. Beat in the melted shortening until combined. In a clean, grease-free bowl, beat the egg whites with an electric mixer or balloon whisk until soft peaks form. Fold one-quarter of the whites into the dough (the dough might be heavy, so take your time), then fold in the remaining whites.

3. Line two rimmed baking sheet pans with a triple layer of paper towels. Heat 3 inches of lard in a deep pot or deep-fat fryer to 350° to 355°F.

4. While the lard is heating, dust the work surface with flour. Scrape the dough onto the surface, dust the top of the dough lightly with flour, and roll out to ⅓-inch thickness (these expand quite a bit). Cut out doughnuts with a lightly floured 3-inch round cutter. Gently gather the scraps, press them together, roll out the dough, and cut out as many additional doughnuts as possible.

5. Fry a few doughnuts at a time; do not crowd. Fry until light golden brown, about 1 minute and 20 seconds, flip them over, and fry for about 1 minute and 20 seconds more, until light golden brown on the other side as well. Using a slotted spoon, remove each doughnut from the lard and drain thoroughly on paper towels. Repeat with the remaining dough.

6. Place the cinnamon-sugar topping and confectioners' sugar in separate wide, shallow bowls. While the doughnuts are still warm, toss half in the cinnamon sugar and half in the confectioners' sugar.

Peach-Pecan Fritters with Brown Sugar Glaze

DESCRIPTION *Small round, moist fritters are dotted with chunks of fresh peaches and chopped pecans. They can be dunked in the brown sugar glaze or it can be drizzled on top.*

FIELD NOTES *Make these when peaches are fragrant and ripe. For a more rustic presentation, you could leave the fruit skin on, although I prefer peeled. Nectarines would make a fine substitution.*

LIFESPAN *These are best eaten as soon as possible.*

Yield: *about 30 golf ball–size fritters*

INGREDIENTS

Brown sugar glaze:
¾ cup firmly packed light brown sugar
6 tablespoons heavy cream
4½ tablespoons unsalted butter
½ teaspoon freshly squeezed lemon juice
Pinch of salt

1 recipe batter for Sour Cream Doughnuts
(page 24)
1½ cups diced (½-inch) peeled peaches
(from about 4 medium peaches)
½ cup pecan halves, chopped
Flavorless vegetable oil for deep-frying,
such as canola

DIRECTIONS

1. *For the glaze:* Place all of the glaze ingredients in a medium-size saucepan and whisk to combine. Bring to a boil over medium heat, whisking occasionally, and boil until the sugar is dissolved and the mixture is smooth, 1 to 2 minutes. Remove from the heat and transfer to a bowl to hasten cooling. Let cool to room temperature; it will thicken slightly.

2. Line a rimmed baking sheet pan with a triple layer of paper towels. Heat 3 inches of oil in a deep pot or deep-fat fryer to 350° to 355°F.

3. While the oil is heating, fold the peaches and pecans into the doughnut batter.

4. Use a 1⅜₁₆-inch ice cream scoop to drop the batter (carefully) into the oil. Alternatively, you can make small rounds by scooping batter with one tablespoon and scraping it off into the oil with another tablespoon. Fry a few fritters at a time; do not crowd. Fry until golden brown, about 1 minute and 40 seconds, flip them over, and fry for about 1 minute and 40 seconds more, until golden brown on the other side as well. Using a slotted spoon, remove each fritter from the oil and drain thoroughly on paper towels. Repeat with the remaining batter.

5. Drizzle the glaze over the fritters or dip each one into the glaze for a more generous amount of topping.

Peanut Butter–Glazed Jelly Doughnuts

DESCRIPTION *A classic jelly-filled doughnut gets a rich, crunchy coating of melted peanut butter and chopped peanuts suspended in a confectioners' sugar glaze. The directions offer you the option of using chunky jam or smooth jelly.*

FIELD NOTES *The Doughnut Plant in New York City has become quite famous for its yeast-raised as well as cake-style doughnuts. It was at their flagship store that I first sampled a jelly doughnut (theirs are square) with a peanut butter glaze. This doughnut has been featured on television shows and hailed as a must-try. I knew I had to take a stab at recreating it for you. If you love PB&J, don't miss this one. Note that the glaze makes enough to coat about 24 doughnuts; depending on the doughnut recipe you choose, you might need more or less glaze. The glaze recipe halves and doubles easily.*

LIFESPAN *These are best eaten as soon as possible.*

Yield: *depends on recipe chosen*

INGREDIENTS

1 recipe Basic Yeast-Raised Doughnuts (page 28), Sweet Cream Doughnuts (page 156), Krispy Kreme Kopykat Doughnuts (page 32), or Chocolate Yeast-Raised Doughnuts (page 30), prepared through the first rise

1¼ to 2¼ cups jam, fruit preserve, or jelly of your choice (I like grape or seedless raspberry; the actual amount depends on the doughnut recipe chosen.)

1½ recipes Peanut Butter Glaze (page 40)

DIRECTIONS

1. Generously flour two rimmed baking sheet pans. Gently punch down the dough and divide it in half.

2. Roll out the dough and either fill then fry the doughnuts (if using a chunky jam) or fry then fill the doughnuts (if using a smooth jelly) as directed in steps 2–4 of Jelly Doughnuts (pages 124–125). Let the doughnuts cool.

3. Line two rimmed baking sheet pans with aluminum foil or parchment paper. Dip the top of each doughnut in the glaze or spread it using a small offset spatula. (If there is extra glaze, dip more of the doughnuts' surface, if you like.) Let the doughnuts sit on the prepared pans until the glaze sets, about 5 minutes.

Pineapple-Filled
Piña Colada Doughnuts

● **DESCRIPTION** *All of the flavors of a piña colada—pineapple, rum, and coconut—*
come together in this doughnut. Yeast-raised doughnuts are filled with pineapple, topped
with rum glaze, and sprinkled with coconut. To make a "virgin" version, substitute
pineapple juice for the rum.

● **FIELD NOTES** *These will knock your socks off! A whole canned pineapple ring is*
embedded inside a ring-shaped raised doughnut and no one will be able to figure out how
you got it in there! Follow the techniques carefully and the results will be impeccable.
It is not difficult; you just have to be precise. You will need two different sizes of
round cutters: 3⅛-inch and ⅞-inch. If you have a complete set of cutters, you will
most likely have these sizes.

● **LIFESPAN** *These are best eaten as soon as possible.*

Yield: *about 14 pineapple-filled doughnuts*

INGREDIENTS

1 recipe Krispy Kreme Kopykat Doughnuts (page 32) or Basic Yeast-Raised Doughnuts (page 28), prepared through the first rise

Two 20-ounce cans pineapple rings, packed in 100% juice (not syrup), drained, juice reserved, and rings patted dry

Flavorless vegetable oil for deep-frying, such as canola

Pineapple rum glaze:

3 tablespoons pineapple juice, reserved from canned pineapple

3 tablespoons golden rum or additional pineapple juice reserved from canned pineapple

3 cups sifted confectioners' sugar

1½ cups lightly packed sweetened long-shred coconut

DIRECTIONS

1. Generously flour two rimmed baking sheet pans. Gently punch down the dough and divide it in half. Roll out one piece on a lightly floured work surface to about ¼-inch thickness. Cut out dough rounds with a lightly floured 3⅛-inch round cutter. Repeat with the remaining dough. Gently gather the scraps, press them together, roll out the dough, and cut out as many additional rounds as possible. Make sure you end up with an even number.

2. This step is very important in order for the doughnuts to work, so take your time. Take a dough round and pat it out so that it is about ¼ inch larger all the way around than the pineapple ring. Place a pineapple ring in the center. Dip a pastry brush in room-temperature water and lightly brush the edges of the dough around the pineapple. Pat out another dough round to stretch it a bit, place it on top of the pineapple, align the edges of the two dough rounds, and use your fingers to press them together and seal the rounds all the way around. Flour the ⅞-inch cutter and cut out the center of the doughnut. Repeat with the remaining dough rounds and pineapple rings.

3. Place the doughnuts, well spaced, on the prepared pans. Let rise in a warm, draft-free location until doubled in size, about 30 minutes.

4. Line two rimmed baking sheet pans with a triple layer of paper towels. Heat 3 inches of oil in a deep pot or deep-fat fryer to 350° to 355°F. When the oil is hot enough, fry a few doughnuts at a time; do not crowd. Fry until light golden brown, about 1½ minutes, flip them over, and fry for about 1½ minutes more, until light golden brown on the other side as well. Using a slotted spoon, remove each doughnut from the oil and drain thoroughly on paper towels. Repeat with the remaining doughnuts. Cool until just barely warm to the touch.

5. *For the glaze*: Whisk together the pineapple juice and rum in a small bowl. Place the confectioners' sugar in a medium bowl and whisk in the liquid, a little bit at a time, until the desired consistency is reached. Dip the top of each doughnut in the glaze and sprinkle generously with the coconut while the glaze is still wet. Let sit for about 5 minutes to allow the glaze to set.

Pumpkin Spice Doughnuts

DESCRIPTION *This cake-style doughnut is gently spiced to allow the pumpkin flavor to shine through. It pairs well with simple glazes and dry toppings.*

FIELD NOTES *Use canned pumpkin puree, not pumpkin pie filling, which is sweetened and spiced. For the photo we drizzled the doughnut with Hard Sugar Glaze (page 34). Feel free to mix and match toppings with this recipe, such as Spiced Orange Glaze (page 36) or a simple Cinnamon-Sugar Topping (page 41).*

LIFESPAN *These are best eaten as soon as possible.*

Yield: *about sixteen 3-inch doughnuts*

INGREDIENTS

3 cups all-purpose flour

1 cup plus 2 tablespoons sifted cake flour

1 tablespoon plus 1 teaspoon baking powder

1 teaspoon ground cinnamon

1 teaspoon salt

½ teaspoon baking soda

½ teaspoon ground ginger

½ teaspoon freshly grated nutmeg

1 cup canned pumpkin puree

2 large eggs, at room temperature

½ cup granulated sugar

½ cup firmly packed light brown sugar

½ cup full-fat sour cream, at room temperature

2 tablespoons flavorless vegetable oil, such as canola, plus more for deep-frying

Glaze(s) or topping(s) of your choice

DIRECTIONS

1. Whisk together both flours, the baking powder, cinnamon, salt, baking soda, ginger, and nutmeg in a medium-size bowl to aerate and combine.

2. In a large bowl, beat together the pumpkin puree, eggs, and both sugars with an electric mixer until creamy, or whisk well by hand. Beat in the sour cream and 2 tablespoons oil until combined. Add the dry mixture in two batches and stir with a wooden spoon just until the dough comes together. Cover and refrigerate for at least 2 hours or up to overnight.

3. Remove the dough from the refrigerator. Line a rimmed baking sheet pan with a triple layer of paper towels. Heat 3 inches of oil in a deep pot or deep-fat fryer to 350° to 355°F.

4. While the oil is heating, dust the work surface with flour. Scrape the dough onto the surface, dust the top of the dough lightly with flour, and roll out to ½-inch thickness. Cut out doughnuts with a lightly floured 3-inch round cutter. Gently gather the scraps, press them together, roll out the dough, and cut out as many additional doughnuts as possible.

5. Fry a few doughnuts at a time; do not crowd. Fry until light golden brown, about 1½ minutes, flip them over, and fry for about 1½ minutes more, until light golden brown on the other side as well. Using a slotted spoon, remove each doughnut from the oil and drain thoroughly on paper towels. Repeat with the remaining dough.

6. While the doughnuts are still slightly warm, apply dry topping(s) or glaze(s) as desired.

Rainbow Sprinkle Doughnuts

DESCRIPTION *This is a classic buttermilk doughnut speckled with multicolored sprinkles (or jimmies, depending on where you live). A simple vanilla glaze topped with additional sprinkles completes the recipe.*

FIELD NOTES *Not surprisingly, kids love these! They are a perfect recipe to make during school vacations or for bake sales. You could also start with Mashed Potato Doughnuts (page 23) or Sour Cream Doughnuts (page 24).*

LIFESPAN *These are best eaten as soon as possible.*

Yield: *about sixteen 3-inch doughnuts*

INGREDIENTS

1 recipe Old-Fashioned Buttermilk Doughnuts (page 22), prepared with 3 tablespoons rainbow sprinkles folded into the batter, cut into 3-inch rings, fried, and beginning to cool

2 recipes Hard Vanilla Glaze (variation of Hard Sugar Glaze, page 34), made immediately before using

Rainbow sprinkles

DIRECTIONS

1. Line two rimmed baking sheet pans with aluminum foil or parchment paper.

2. Dip the top of each doughnut into the glaze and generously scatter sprinkles on top of the glaze before it sets. Let the doughnuts sit on the prepared pans until the glaze sets, about 5 minutes.

Raspberry–Crème Fraîche Doughnuts

DESCRIPTION *This yeast-raised doughnut is filled with both a dollop of crème fraîche and fresh raspberries.*

FIELD NOTES *Crème fraîche is a cultured dairy product similar to sour cream, but much more nuanced, complex, and elegant in flavor. You can find it in cheese stores as well as in the cheese department or dairy section of better supermarkets. I like Vermont Butter & Cheese Creamery brand for its reliably thick consistency and brilliant white color. You could toss the doughnuts in regular granulated sugar, but superfine sugar gives them a delicate look and crunch. It is sold in boxes near the regular sugar in the baking aisle.*

LIFESPAN *These are best eaten as soon as possible.*

Yield: *about twenty-six 2½-inch filled doughnuts*

INGREDIENTS

1 recipe Krispy Kreme Kopykat Doughnuts (page 32) or Basic Yeast-Raised Doughnuts (page 28), prepared through the first rise

1¼ cups crème fraîche

1 pint fresh raspberries (You will need 50 to 80 raspberries, depending on their size.)

Flavorless vegetable oil for deep-frying, such as canola

Superfine sugar

DIRECTIONS

1. Generously flour two rimmed baking sheet pans. Gently punch down the dough and divide it in half. Roll out one piece of dough on a lightly floured work surface to ¼-inch thickness. Cut out dough rounds with a lightly floured 2½-inch round cutter. Repeat with the remaining dough. Gently gather the scraps, press them together, roll out the dough, and cut out as many additional rounds as possible. Make sure you end up with an even number.

2. Using two cereal spoons, dollop about 2 teaspoons of crème fraîche in the centers of half of the dough rounds. Press 2 or 3 raspberries (depending on their size) into the crème fraîche. Dip a pastry brush in room-temperature water and lightly brush the edges of the dough around the filling. Place a plain round on top of each filled round and press the edges together with your fingertips to seal them well.

3. Place the doughnuts, well spaced, on the prepared pans. Let rise in a warm, draft-free location until doubled in size, about 30 minutes.

4. Line two rimmed baking sheet pans with a triple layer of paper towels. Heat 3 inches of oil in a deep pot or deep-fat fryer to 350° to 355°F. When the oil is hot enough, fry a few doughnuts at a time; do not crowd. Fry until light golden brown, about 1½ minutes, flip them over, and fry for about 1½ minutes more, until light golden brown on the other side as well. Using a slotted spoon, remove each doughnut from the oil and drain thoroughly on paper towels. Repeat with the remaining doughnuts. Cool until barely warm.

5. Toss the doughnuts in superfine sugar to coat completely.

Red Velvet Doughnuts

○ **DESCRIPTION** *These fried red velvet doughnuts have the traditional red color and subtle cocoa flavor. Cream cheese frosting is slathered on top.*

○ **FIELD NOTES** *Red velvet batter has a lot of red food coloring and actually just a bit of cocoa; it is not a very chocolatey flavor, but you can't keep the fans away. Cream cheese frosting is expected, so I have included it here, but don't shy away from trying Dark Chocolate Ganache Glaze (page 39) or any of the chocolate glazes. Chocolate doughnuts are so dark that it is hard to tell when they are done; frying and testing a sample doughnut is a must.*

○ **LIFESPAN** *These are best eaten as soon as possible.*

Yield: *about nine 3-inch doughnuts*

INGREDIENTS

1¾ cups plus 3 tablespoons all-purpose flour
¾ cup sifted cake flour
¾ cup sugar
2 tablespoons sifted Dutch-processed cocoa powder
2 teaspoons baking powder
1 teaspoon salt
¼ teaspoon baking soda
1 large egg, at room temperature

2 large egg yolks, at room temperature
¾ cup buttermilk, at room temperature
3 tablespoons unsalted butter, melted and cooled
1 teaspoon red food coloring (gel or liquid)
½ teaspoon pure vanilla extract
Flavorless vegetable oil for deep-frying, such as canola
Half a recipe Cream Cheese Frosting (page 41)

DIRECTIONS

1. Whisk together both flours, the sugar, cocoa, baking powder, salt, and baking soda in a small bowl to aerate and combine.

2. In a large bowl, beat together the whole egg and egg yolks with an electric mixer until pale and creamy, or whisk well by hand. Beat in the buttermilk, melted butter, food coloring, and vanilla until combined. Add the dry mixture in two batches and stir with a wooden spoon just until the dough comes together. Cover and refrigerate for at least 2 hours or up to overnight.

3. Remove the dough from the refrigerator. Line a rimmed baking sheet pan with a triple layer of paper towels. Heat 3 inches of oil in a deep pot or deep-fat fryer to 350° to 355°F.

4. While the oil is heating, dust the work surface liberally with flour. Scrape the dough onto the surface, dust the top of the dough lightly with flour, and roll out to ½-inch thickness. Cut out doughnuts with a lightly floured 3-inch round cutter. Gently gather the scraps, press them together, roll out the dough, and cut out as many additional doughnuts as possible.

5. Fry a few doughnuts at a time; do not crowd. Fry about 1 minute and 40 seconds, flip them over, and fry for about 1 minute and 40 seconds more, until just cooked through. Using a slotted spoon, remove each doughnut from the oil and drain thoroughly on paper towels. Repeat with the remaining dough.

6. While the doughnuts are still barely warm, spread the tops with the frosting, using a small offset spatula.

Rich Yeast-Raised Doughnuts

 **DESCRIPTION** *Egg yolk–rich, these doughnuts have a beautiful golden color and are highly flavored with vanilla, making them more flavorful than my Basic Yeast-Raised Doughnuts (page 28). The dough has a lot of character unto itself—it's almost like a brioche.*

 **FIELD NOTES** *Not all yeast-raised doughnuts are created equal. Some function more as a light, chewy backdrop for their fillings, while others, such as these, are more of an all-around pastry. Mix and match with the fillings and toppings of your choice.*

 **LIFESPAN** *These are best eaten as soon as possible.*

Yield: *about eighteen 2½-inch filled round doughnuts or about sixteen 3-inch ring-shaped doughnuts*

INGREDIENTS

¾ cup warm milk (110° to 115°F)
One 0.25-ounce package active dry yeast
½ cup (1 stick) unsalted butter, melted and cooled slightly
½ cup sugar
7 large egg yolks, at room temperature, beaten

2 tablespoons pure vanilla extract
1 teaspoon salt
3 to 3¼ cups all-purpose flour
Flavorless vegetable oil for deep-frying, such as canola
Filling(s), topping(s), and/or glaze(s) of choice

DIRECTIONS

1. Place the warm milk in a large bowl and sprinkle the yeast over it. Stir to combine and let sit for 5 minutes. Meanwhile, whisk together the melted butter, sugar, egg yolks, vanilla, and salt in a medium-size bowl.

2. Whisk the egg yolk mixture into the yeast mixture. Stir in 3 cups of the flour; the mixture will be very wet. If using a stand mixer, attach the dough hook and mix until the dough is combined and elastic, about 2 minutes. You can also do this by hand with a wooden spoon, beating vigorously for several minutes. Add additional flour, 1 tablespoon at a time, only if needed to create a soft, elastic dough that is still slightly sticky.

3. Scrape the dough into a buttered bowl, making sure there is plenty of headroom. Cover the bowl with plastic wrap and place in a warm, draft-free location to rise until doubled in size, about 2 hours.

4. Gently deflate the dough, gather it into a ball again, cover with plastic again, and let rise for another 30 minutes.

5. Generously flour two rimmed baking sheet pans. Gently punch down the dough and divide it in half. Roll out one piece of dough on a lightly floured work surface to ½-inch thickness. Cut out doughnuts with a lightly floured cutter. Use a 2½-inch round cutter for filled doughnuts or a 3-inch ring-shaped cutter for a classic doughnut shape. Repeat with the remaining dough. Gently gather the scraps, press them together, roll out the dough, and cut out as many additional doughnuts as possible. Place the doughnuts, well spaced, on the prepared pans. Let rise in a warm, draft-free location for about 30 minutes.

6. Line two rimmed baking sheet pans with a triple layer of paper towels. Heat 3 inches of oil in a deep pot or deep-fat fryer to 350° to 355°F. When the oil is hot enough, fry a few doughnuts at a time; do not crowd. Fry until light golden brown, about 1½ minutes, flip them over, and fry for about 1½ minutes more, until light golden brown on the other side as well. Using a slotted spoon, remove each doughnut from the oil and drain thoroughly on paper towels. Repeat with the remaining doughnuts.

7. Insert the filling(s) and/or apply dry topping(s) or glaze(s) as desired.

Ricotta Fritters

DESCRIPTION *Small and light, these fritters are heavily dusted with confectioners' sugar. You can make them in sizes ranging from large olives to golf balls.*

FIELD NOTES *This is a classic Italian fried dough dessert. Some recipes do not include sugar or lemon zest, but I prefer to add both. The overall flavor is delicate, but the additional flavorings add oomph. Most recipes call for all-purpose flour, but I find that the use of cake flour makes these positively ethereal in texture. Sometimes referred to as* zeppole, *these fritters are often served in Italy for St. Joseph's Day (March 19).*

LIFESPAN *These are best eaten as soon as possible.*

Ⓒ ⏱ ☺

Yield: *about 25 small fritters*

INGREDIENTS

1 cup whole-milk ricotta
¼ cup granulated sugar
2 large eggs, at room temperature
1 teaspoon finely grated lemon zest
½ teaspoon pure vanilla extract
Pinch of salt

¾ cup sifted cake flour
1 ½ teaspoons baking powder
Flavorless vegetable oil for deep-frying,
   such as canola
Confectioners' sugar

DIRECTIONS

1. Line a rimmed baking sheet pan with a triple layer of paper towels. Heat 3 inches of oil in a deep pot or deep-fat fryer to 350° to 355°F.

2. While the oil is heating, whisk together the ricotta, granulated sugar, eggs, lemon zest, vanilla, and salt in a medium-size bowl until smooth. Whisk in the flour and baking powder.

3. Use a 1-inch ice cream scoop to drop the batter (carefully) into the hot oil. Alternatively, you can make small rounds by scooping a bit of dough with one teaspoon and scraping it off into the oil with another teaspoon.

Fry a few at a time; do not crowd. Fry until golden brown, about 1 minute, flip them over, and fry for about 1 minute more, until golden brown on the other side as well. Using a slotted spoon, remove each fritter from the oil and drain thoroughly on paper towels. Repeat with the remaining dough.

4. While they are still warm, coat the fritters heavily with confectioners' sugar. You can sift the sugar over them on a baking sheet pan, then roll them in excess confectioners' sugar on all sides, or you can gently toss them in a bowl or a bag of confectioners' sugar.

Rose Petal French Crullers

DESCRIPTION *Light, airy, crisp French crullers are brushed with a rose water glaze and sprinkled with edible rose petals.*

FIELD NOTES *The Doughnut Plant in New York City often offers a doughnut covered in a sticky glaze to which rose petals cling. It is beautiful, but I find the texture of the doughnut to be heavier than what I think is appropriate for such an ethereal concept. The use of French crullers as a base, in my opinion, raises this doughnut to even greater heights of delectability. Rose water can be found in specialty stores or the international aisle of some supermarkets. Roses are edible, but pesticides are not—find unsprayed roses from a home garden, farmer's market, or other reliable source.*

LIFESPAN *These are best eaten as soon as possible.*

Yield: *about nine 3-inch crullers*

INGREDIENTS

Rose water glaze:
  1 cup sifted confectioners' sugar
  2 tablespoons milk
  2 teaspoons rose water

1 recipe French Crullers (page 25), fried
  and beginning to cool
Fresh pesticide-free rose petals

DIRECTIONS

Whisk together the confectioners'
sugar, milk, and rose water in a small
bowl until smooth. Immediately apply
the glaze all over the tops of the crullers with a pastry brush or dip the tops
in the glaze. Sprinkle with rose petals
while the glaze is still wet. Let sit for
5 minutes to allow the glaze to set.

Spiced Chocolate Doughnuts

 **DESCRIPTION** *This chocolate cake doughnut is enlivened with cinnamon, nutmeg, cardamom, cloves, and ginger in both the dough and the sparkly sugar topping.*

 **FIELD NOTES** *These offer a twist on the expected flavors that usually accompany chocolate. For chocolate doughnut fans, they are a nice addition to your repertoire. I particularly love having one with a cup of steaming-hot milky black tea. If you like spicy hot, add the optional cayenne.*

 **LIFESPAN** *These are best eaten as soon as possible.*

Yield: *about fourteen 3-inch doughnuts*

INGREDIENTS

1 recipe Chocolate Cake-Style Doughnuts (page 26), prepared adding 1 teaspoon each ground cinnamon and freshly grated nutmeg and ½ teaspoon each ground cardamom, ground cloves, ground ginger, and cayenne pepper (optional) to the dry mixture, cut into 3-inch rings, fried, and beginning to cool

1 recipe Cinnamon-Sugar Topping (page 41), prepared adding ½ teaspoon ground cardamom

DIRECTIONS

While they are still slightly warm, roll the doughnuts on all sides in the cinnamon-sugar-cardamom topping.

Sweet Cream Doughnuts

DESCRIPTION *This springy, tender yeast-raised doughnut has an almost brioche-like flavor.*

FIELD NOTES *I found a recipe by this name in an e-book by Peter Ruble called* 173 Recipes for Homemade Doughnuts. *The ingredients and technique were unlike anything I had ever seen in a doughnut recipe, so I had to try it. I increased the salt and added egg yolk, vanilla, and nutmeg (still yielding a very neutral-flavored doughnut), and my testing required twice as much flour as his recipe suggested. This is an adapted recipe, but you will still follow the original—and very unusual—technique of pouring boiling water over heavy cream. Kids who are familiar with more classic baking techniques will find this fascinating, as do I.*

LIFESPAN *These are best eaten as soon as possible.*

:)

Yield: *about thirty-six 2½-inch filled round doughnuts or about thirty 3-inch ring-shaped doughnuts*

INGREDIENTS

¼ cup warm water (110° to 115°F)
One 0.25-ounce package active dry yeast
½ cup flavorless vegetable oil, such as canola, plus more for deep-frying
½ cup heavy cream
6 tablespoons sugar
½ teaspoon salt
½ teaspoon freshly grated nutmeg

½ teaspoon pure vanilla extract
2½ cups boiling water
3 large egg yolks, well beaten
8 to 9 cups all-purpose flour, plus more if needed
Filling(s), topping(s), and/or glaze(s) of choice

DIRECTIONS

1. Place the warm water in a small bowl and sprinkle the yeast over it. Stir to combine and let sit for 5 minutes.

2. Place ½ cup oil, the cream, sugar, salt, nutmeg, and vanilla in a large heat-proof bowl. Pour the boiling water over the oil-cream mixture, whisk to combine, and let cool to lukewarm.

3. Whisk the yeast mixture and beaten egg yolks into the lukewarm mixture. Add the flour gradually until a soft, slightly sticky, elastic dough forms. Knead well by hand or use the dough hook of a stand mixer. Knead until the dough is elastic and pulls away from the sides of the bowl with a little help from a spatula. (It might still be a bit sticky and not come off cleanly on its own; do not add more flour or the doughnuts will be dry.)

4. Scrape the dough into a buttered bowl, making sure there is plenty of head-room. Cover the bowl with plastic wrap and place in a warm, draft-free location to rise until doubled in size, about 2 hours.

5. Generously flour three rimmed baking sheet pans. Gently punch down the dough and divide it into fourths. Roll out one piece of dough on a lightly floured work surface to ½-inch thickness. Cut out doughnuts with a lightly floured cutter. Use a 2½-inch round cutter for filled doughnuts or a 3-inch ring-shaped doughnut cutter for a classic doughnut shape. Repeat with the remaining dough. Gently gather the scraps, press them together, roll out the dough, and cut out as many additional rounds as possible. Place the doughnuts, well spaced, on the prepared pans. Let rise in a warm, draft-free location for 30 minutes.

6. Line three rimmed baking sheet pans with a triple layer of paper towels. Heat 3 inches of oil in a deep pot or deep-fat fryer to 350° to 355°F. When the oil is hot enough, fry a few doughnuts at a time; do not crowd. Fry until light golden brown, about 1 minute and 15 seconds, flip them over, and fry for about 1 minute and 15 seconds more, until light golden brown on the other side. Using a slotted spoon, remove each doughnut from the oil and drain thoroughly on paper towels. Repeat with remaining doughnuts.

7. Insert filling(s) and/or apply dry topping(s) or glaze(s) as desired.

Sweet Potato Doughnuts

 **DESCRIPTION** *Crisp outside and tender inside, these doughnuts have a slightly dense, velvety crumb. The sweet potato adds vibrant color, rich texture, and a mild, sweet flavor. These doughnuts pair with many toppings and glazes; I suggest Cinnamon-Sugar Topping (page 41) as well as Citrus Glaze (page 35) made with orange juice.*

 **FIELD NOTES** *I like to use deep orange-colored sweet potatoes to give the finished doughnut extra color, which I do think is part of its charm. You can either bake the sweet potato or microwave it on the "baked potato" setting. I use a pastry blender to mash it finely before measuring.*

 **LIFESPAN** *These are best eaten as soon as possible.*

Yield: *about twelve 3-inch doughnuts*

INGREDIENTS

2½ cups all-purpose flour
1 cup sifted cake flour
2 teaspoons baking powder
¾ teaspoon salt
½ teaspoon baking soda
½ teaspoon ground cinnamon
¼ teaspoon freshly grated nutmeg
1 cup sugar
2 large eggs, at room temperature

1 cup lightly packed mashed sweet potato, cooled (see Field Notes)
1 cup full-fat sour cream, at room temperature
1 teaspoon pure vanilla extract
Flavorless vegetable oil for deep-frying, such as canola
Topping(s) and/or glaze(s) of choice

DIRECTIONS

1. Whisk together both flours, the baking powder, salt, baking soda, cinnamon, and nutmeg in a medium-size bowl to aerate and combine.

2. In a large bowl, beat together the sugar and eggs with an electric mixer until pale and creamy, or whisk well by hand. Beat in the mashed sweet potato, sour cream, and vanilla just until combined. Add the dry mixture in two batches and stir with a wooden spoon just until the dough comes together. Cover and refrigerate for at least 2 hours or up to overnight.

3. Remove the dough from the refrigerator. Line a rimmed baking sheet pan with a triple layer of paper towels. Heat 3 inches of oil in a deep pot or deep-fat fryer to 350° to 355°F.

4. While the oil is heating, dust the work surface generously with flour. Scrape the dough onto the surface, dust the top of the dough lightly with flour, and roll out to ½-inch thickness. Cut out doughnuts with a lightly floured 3-inch round cutter. Gently gather the scraps, press them together, roll out the dough, and cut out as many additional doughnuts as possible.

5. Fry a few doughnuts at a time; do not crowd. Fry until light golden brown, about 1½ minutes, flip them over, and fry for about 1½ minutes more, until light golden brown on the other side as well. Using a slotted spoon, remove each doughnut from the oil and drain thoroughly on paper towels. Repeat with the remaining doughnuts.

6. Apply dry topping(s) or glaze(s) as desired.

Toasted Almond Doughnuts

DESCRIPTION *Yeast-raised doughnuts are filled with almond paste, drenched in almond glaze, and sprinkled with caramelized almonds for a triple-almond delight.*

FIELD NOTES *I absolutely love the flavor of almond paste and was determined to work it into a doughnut. If you like almond-filled Danish pastries, these will appeal to you. I use American Almond brand almond paste, which can be found at King Arthur Flour (see Resources, page 173). Note that the caramelized almonds can be made several days ahead of time, as long as you store them in an airtight container away from any humidity.*

LIFESPAN *These are best eaten as soon as possible.*

Yield: *about twenty-eight 2½-inch doughnuts*

INGREDIENTS

Caramelized almonds:

2 cups sugar

½ cup water

2⅔ cups slivered or sliced blanched
almonds, roughly chopped

1 recipe Krispy Kreme Kopykat Doughnuts
(page 32) or Basic Yeast-Raised

Doughnuts (page 28), prepared through
the first rise

22 ounces almond paste

2 recipes Soft and Sheer Almond Glaze
(variation of Soft and Sheer Sugar Glaze,
page 35)

Flavorless vegetable oil for deep-frying,
such as canola

DIRECTIONS

1. *For the caramelized almonds:* Line a rimmed baking sheet pan with parchment paper or aluminum foil and coat with nonstick cooking spray. Stir the sugar and water together in a large saucepan. Bring to a simmer over medium-high heat, swirling the pan once or twice, but do not stir. Cook (again, without stirring) until the sugar is caramelized and has turned a medium golden brown. Stir in the almonds until coated, then immediately scrape them out onto the prepared pan. Cool and chop finely. This can be done up to 4 days ahead; store in an airtight container at room temperature.

2. Generously flour two rimmed baking sheet pans. Gently punch down the dough and divide it in half. Roll out one piece of dough on a lightly floured work surface to ¼-inch thickness. Cut out dough rounds with a lightly floured 2½-inch round cutter. Repeat with the remaining dough. Gather the scraps, press them together, roll out the dough, and cut out as many additional rounds as possible. Make sure you end up with an even number.

3. Take walnut-sized chunks of almond paste and flatten them into disks about ¼ inch thick. Place the almond paste

disks in the centers of half of the dough rounds. Dip a pastry brush in room-temperature water and lightly brush the edges of the dough around the almond paste. Place a plain round on top of each filled round and press the edges together with your fingertips to seal them well.

4. Place the doughnuts, well spaced, on the prepared pans. Let rise in a warm, draft-free location until doubled in size, about 30 minutes.

5. Line two rimmed baking sheet pans with a triple layer of paper towels. Heat 3 inches of oil in a deep pot or deep-fat fryer to 350° to 355°F. When the oil is hot enough, fry a few doughnuts at a time; do not crowd. Fry until light golden brown, about 1½ minutes, flip them over, and fry for about 1½ minutes more, until light golden brown on the other side. Using a slotted spoon, remove each doughnut from the oil and drain thoroughly on paper towels. Repeat with remaining doughnuts.

6. While the doughnuts are still slightly warm, dip the tops in the glaze. Sprinkle the almonds on top while the glaze is still wet. Let sit for about 5 minutes to allow the glaze to set.

Toffee Crunch
Chocolate Ganache Doughnuts

DESCRIPTION *These are sour cream doughnuts with toffee bits and semisweet chocolate chips folded into the dough. After cooling, the tops are slathered with dark chocolate ganache and sprinkled with more toffee bits.*

FIELD NOTES *I use Heath Bits 'O Brickle or Skor Toffee Bits; they are easy to find in most supermarkets. Just make sure to use plain toffee bits and not chocolate-covered toffee bits (which are delicious, but not what is called for here). You will have some leftover ganache, which is heavenly melted over ice cream. In the winter, I like to place a dollop of ganache in a mug with milk and microwave for instant hot chocolate!*

LIFESPAN *These are best eaten as soon as possible.*

Yield: *about twelve 3-inch doughnuts*

INGREDIENTS

1 recipe Sour Cream Doughnuts (page 24), prepared folding 1 cup each miniature semisweet chocolate morsels and toffee bits (such as Heath Bits 'O Brickle) into the final dough, cut into 3-inch rings, fried, and beginning to cool

1 recipe Dark Chocolate Ganache Glaze (page 39)
⅔ cup toffee bits

DIRECTIONS

While the doughnuts are still slightly warm, dip the tops in the glaze. Sprinkle generously with the toffee bits while the glaze is still wet. Let sit for about 5 minutes to allow the glaze to set.

Vanilla Bean Custard Doughnuts

 **DESCRIPTION** *These yeast-raised doughnuts are filled with vanilla pastry cream and covered with a vanilla glaze for tons of vanilla flavor.*

 **FIELD NOTES** *You will need vanilla extract and vanilla beans for this recipe. Use pure vanilla extract for the best flavor; I like Nielsen-Massey brand. When shopping for vanilla beans, look for soft, plump, moist beans. They should look shiny and be pliable, if you can feel them (sometimes they are in a glass container). Bourbon beans, by the way, are a type of vanilla bean and have nothing to do with the whiskey.*

 **LIFESPAN** *These are best eaten as soon as possible.*

C

Yield: *about twenty-eight 2½-inch filled doughnuts*

INGREDIENTS

1 recipe Rich Vanilla Pastry Cream
(variation of Pastry Cream, page 42)
1 recipe Krispy Kreme Kopykat Doughnuts
(page 32) or Basic Yeast-Raised
Doughnuts (page 28), cut into 2½-inch
rounds, fried, and beginning to cool
1 plump, moist vanilla bean

2 recipes Soft and Sheer Vanilla Glaze
(variation of Soft and Sheer Sugar Glaze,
page 35)

Pastry bag and coupler fitted with a
Bismarck #230 tip

DIRECTIONS

1. Scrape the pastry cream into the pastry bag. Insert the tip into the side of a cooled doughnut. Squeeze the pastry bag and fill the doughnut with pastry cream just until the center of the doughnut slightly bulges. (You are aiming to pipe a generous 2 to 3 teaspoons of filling inside.) Repeat with the remaining doughnuts and pastry cream.

2. Slit the vanilla bean lengthwise and use a butter knife or teaspoon to scrape all of the tiny seeds into the glaze. Whisk until the seeds are evenly dispersed.

3. Dip the top of each doughnut in the glaze and let sit for about 5 minutes to allow the glaze to set.

Vegan Gluten-Free Baked Doughnuts

DESCRIPTION *These soft, moist baked doughnuts just happen to be gluten free and vegan. Top or glaze as you like; I suggest keeping it simple with cinnamon sugar.*

FIELD NOTES *Applesauce lends moisture to these doughnuts, which are based on a recipe from* BabyCakes Covers the Classics *(Clarkson Potter, 2011). I have tweaked both the ingredients and the technique. If you are ever in New York and are a fan of gluten-free baked goods, make a beeline for BabyCakes NYC. Vegan sugar is called for, as some refined sugar is processed with an animal by-product called bone char. It all depends on how strict a vegan you are (or are serving); many vegans eat regular granulated sugar. Xanthan gum is a common ingredient used when baking gluten-free. It helps create a tender texture in the absence of gluten and is a vital ingredient. You can find it at Whole Foods Market or wherever you shop for gluten-free baking ingredients.*

LIFESPAN *These are best eaten the day they are made.*

Yield: *twelve 3½-inch doughnuts*

INGREDIENTS

1¾ cups plus 2 tablespoons sifted gluten-
  free baking mix, such as Bob's Red Mill
  All-Purpose Baking Flour
1½ teaspoons baking powder
½ teaspoon salt
½ teaspoon xanthan gum
¼ teaspoon freshly grated nutmeg

⅛ teaspoon baking soda
¾ cup plus 2 tablespoons vegan sugar
½ cup hot water
⅓ cup unsweetened applesauce
3 tablespoons pure vanilla extract
Half a recipe Cinnamon-Sugar Topping
  (page 41), made with vegan sugar

DIRECTIONS

1. Position a rack in the middle of the oven. Preheat the oven to 325°F. Coat two standard-sized doughnut pans (12 wells total) with nonstick cooking spray.

2. Whisk together the flour, baking powder, salt, xanthan gum, nutmeg, and baking soda in a large bowl to aerate and combine.

3. Whisk together the sugar, water, applesauce, and vanilla in a medium-size bowl. Pour the wet ingredients over the dry mixture and fold together with a wooden spoon just until combined and smooth. Divide the batter evenly among the wells of the prepared pans. Use a small offset spatula to spread the batter evenly, if necessary.

4. Bake until a toothpick inserted in the center of a doughnut shows a few moist crumbs when removed, about 12 minutes. Cool the pans on racks for about 5 minutes, and then unmold the doughnuts directly onto the racks.

5. While the doughnuts are still warm, toss them in the cinnamon sugar until completely coated.

White Chocolate
Truffle Doughnuts

 **DESCRIPTION** *This is a cake-style doughnut dipped into a white chocolate ganache glaze (just like a melted truffle) and covered with white chocolate curls.*

 **FIELD NOTES** *White chocolate isn't chocolate at all, according to the FDA, as it doesn't contain any cacao mass from the cacao bean. High-quality white chocolate will, however, have cocoa butter listed as its fat. No other fat, such as cottonseed oil or palm oil, should be listed. I highly recommend Valrhona Ivoire for the best flavor and texture.*

 **LIFESPAN** *These are best eaten as soon as possible.*

Yield: *depends on doughnut recipe chosen; glaze recipe makes enough to coat twenty 3-inch doughnuts*

INGREDIENTS

One 6-ounce block white chocolate, such as Valrhona Ivoire or Callebaut

White chocolate truffle glaze:
¾ cup heavy cream
21 ounces white chocolate, such as Valrhona Ivoire or Callebaut, finely chopped

1 recipe Sour Cream Doughnuts (page 24), Old-Fashioned Buttermilk Doughnuts (page 22), or Chocolate Cake-Style Doughnuts (page 26), cut into 3-inch rings, fried, and beginning to cool

DIRECTIONS

1. Use a sharp vegetable peeler to shave small curls off the block of chocolate directly into an airtight plastic container. These may be made a few days ahead and refrigerated.

2. Line two rimmed baking sheet pans with aluminum foil or parchment paper.

3. *For the glaze*: Bring the cream to a simmer in a 2-quart wide saucepan over medium heat. Remove from the heat and immediately sprinkle the chopped chocolate into the cream. Cover and let sit for 5 minutes. Gently stir the ganache until smooth—the heat of the cream should melt the chocolate. If the chocolate does not melt completely, place the pan over very low heat and stir the ganache often, until it is melted, taking care not to burn it. Cool until warm but still fluid. (You may hasten the cooling process by stirring the ganache over an ice bath. If it becomes too firm, or if you would like to return it to a softer state, simply place it over hot water or microwave it briefly.)

4. Pour the cooled glaze into a wide, shallow bowl. While the doughnuts are still slightly warm, dip the tops in the glaze or spread the glaze using a small offset spatula. Sprinkle the glazed side generously with the white chocolate curls while the ganache is cool but still a bit sticky. Let sit for about 5 minutes to allow the glaze to set.

Walnut Streusel–Sour Cream Doughnuts with Maple Glaze

DESCRIPTION *These cinnamon-spiked sour cream doughnuts are brushed with a maple glaze and topped with nutty, crunchy streusel.*

FIELD NOTES *A version of these first appeared in* Bon Appétit *magazine in October 2004. They are the very first doughnuts I ever created, so I thought they deserved a reprise here.*

LIFESPAN *These are best eaten as soon as possible.*

Yield: *about twenty-four 2½-inch doughnuts*

INGREDIENTS

Walnut streusel:
- I large egg white
- ¼ cup granulated sugar
- I teaspoon ground cinnamon
- I ½ cups walnut halves, finely chopped

Doughnuts:
- 2½ cups all-purpose flour
- I cup plus I tablespoon sifted cake flour
- I tablespoon baking powder
- I teaspoon ground cinnamon
- I teaspoon salt
- ½ teaspoon baking soda
- I cup granulated sugar

- 2 large eggs, at room temperature
- 6 tablespoons (¾ stick) unsalted butter, melted and cooled
- I cup full-fat sour cream, at room temperature
- I teaspoon pure vanilla extract
- Flavorless vegetable oil for deep-frying, such as canola

Maple glaze:
- 2 cups sifted confectioners' sugar
- 3 tablespoons pure maple syrup
- 4 tablespoons water

DIRECTIONS

1. *For the streusel:* Preheat the oven to 325°F. Line a rimmed baking sheet pan with parchment paper. Whisk the egg white in a small bowl until frothy. Whisk in the granulated sugar and cinnamon; fold in the nuts. Spread the mixture on the prepared pan in a thin, even layer. Bake until the mixture is beginning to dry, about 10 minutes. Stir to break up the nuts. Continue to bake until the nut mixture is golden brown, about 5 minutes more. Cool the pan completely on a rack. Transfer the streusel to a cutting board and chop very finely. Transfer to a wide, shallow bowl.

2. *For the doughnuts:* Whisk together both flours, the baking powder, cinnamon, salt, and baking soda in a medium-size bowl to aerate and combine.

3. In a large bowl, beat together the granulated sugar and eggs with an electric mixer on medium-high speed until pale and creamy, or whisk well by

hand. Beat in the melted butter, sour cream, and vanilla until combined. Add the dry mixture in two batches and stir with a wooden spoon just until the dough comes together. Cover and refrigerate for at least 2 hours or up to overnight.

4. Remove the dough from the refrigerator. Line two rimmed baking sheet pans with a triple layer of paper towels. Heat 3 inches of oil in a deep pot or deep-fat fryer to 350° to 355°F.

5. While the oil is heating, dust the work surface with flour. Scrape the dough onto the surface, dust the top of the dough lightly with flour, and roll out to ¾-inch thickness. Cut out doughnuts with a lightly floured 2½-inch round cutter. Gently gather the scraps, press them together, and cut out as many additional doughnuts as possible.

6. Fry a few doughnuts at a time; do not crowd. Fry until light golden brown, about 1 minute, flip them over, and fry

for about 1 minute more, until light golden brown on the other side as well. Using a slotted spoon, remove each doughnut from the oil and drain thoroughly on paper towels. Repeat with the remaining dough.

7. *For the glaze*: Combine the confectioners' sugar and maple syrup in a small saucepan. Add 3 tablespoons of the water and whisk until smooth, adding the remaining 1 tablespoon water if necessary to make a thick but smooth and pourable glaze. Heat the mixture gently over low heat until very warm to the touch but not hot. Remove from the heat and scrape into a wide, shallow bowl.

8. While the doughnuts are still slightly warm, dip the tops in the glaze, then quickly dip the glazed side into the streusel. Arrange the doughnuts, streusel side up, on a rack for at least 30 minutes or longer if needed to set the glaze and topping.

Resources

Beryl's Cake Decorating and Pastry Supplies
P.O. Box 1584
North Springfield, VA 22151
(800) 488-2749
(703) 256-6951
Fax (703) 750-3779
beryls.com

There is a Beryl, and she will often answer the phone herself. Look here for high-quality baking pans and tools, pastry bags and tips, sugar decorations, blocks of caramel, and more. Peruse this voluminous website for your baking and decorating needs.

Chocosphere
(877) 992-4626
Fax (877) 912-4626
chocosphere.com

If you are looking for high-quality chocolate or gianduja, order from this fabulous mail-order company. They specialize in all my favorite chocolates that are great to eat and to use in your baked goods. Owners Joanne and Jerry Kryszek offer excellent personal service, and they ship nationwide.

Just Tomatoes, Etc.!
P.O. Box 807
Westley, CA 95387
(800) 537-1985
(209) 894-5371
Fax (209) 894-3146
justtomatoes.com

This company makes freeze-dried fruits and vegetables that are crisp and colorful and have very true flavor. The fruits, such as strawberries, raspberries, bananas, blackberries, cherries, and blueberries, add color and flavor to doughnuts, especially as decoration. You can order them direct or look for them in specialty stores and Whole Foods Market. Look for the dried strawberries in the Chocolate-Covered Strawberry Doughnuts (page 80).

King Arthur Flour
P.O. Box 876
Norwich, VT 05055
(800) 827-6836
(802) 649-3881
Fax (800) 343-3002
kingarthurflour.com

This catalog and website offers high-quality flours, extracts, chocolates, bulk caramel, instant espresso powder, scales, measuring cups (including handy ones in odd sizes), Zeroll scoops, doughnut pans, and more. As always, my recipes are tested with King Arthur Unbleached All-Purpose Flour.

Sur La Table
P.O. Box 840
Brownsburg, IN 46112
(800) 243-0852
Fax (317) 858-5521
surlatable.com

This fabulous mail-order company also has stores throughout the country. They have a great selection of KitchenAid mixers, baking pans, silicone spatulas, measuring implements, mixing bowls, chocolate, cocoa powder, lovely serving pieces, and much more.

Williams-Sonoma
3250 Van Ness Avenue
San Francisco, CA 94109
(877) 812-6235
Fax (702) 363-2541
williams-sonoma.com

This well-known company offers quality baking pans, tools, some ingredients, KitchenAid mixers, measuring implements, and more.

Zeroll Products
P.O. Box 999
Fort Pierce, FL 34954
(800) USA-5000
zeroll.com

This company makes the best ice cream scoops. They call them Universal EZ Dishers on the site, and they come in many sizes. I use the #40 for my standard doughnut holes.

Measurement Equivalents

Please note that all conversions are approximate.

Liquid Conversions

U.S.	Metric
1 tsp	5 ml
1 tbs	15 ml
2 tbs	30 ml
3 tbs	45 ml
$^1/_4$ cup	60 ml
$^1/_3$ cup	75 ml
$^1/_3$ cup + 1 tbs	90 ml
$^1/_3$ cup + 2 tbs	100 ml
$^1/_2$ cup	120 ml
$^2/_3$ cup	150 ml
$^3/_4$ cup	180 ml
$^3/_4$ cup + 2 tbs	200 ml
1 cup	240 ml
1 cup + 2 tbs	275 ml
$1^1/_4$ cups	300 ml
$1^1/_3$ cups	325 ml
$1^1/_2$ cups	350 ml
$1^2/_3$ cups	375 ml
$1^3/_4$ cups	400 ml
$1^3/_4$ cups + 2 tbs	450 ml
2 cups (1 pint)	475 ml
$2^1/_2$ cups	600 ml
3 cups	720 ml
4 cups (1 quart)	945 ml (1,000 ml is 1 liter)

Weight Conversions

US/UK	Metric
$^1/_2$ oz	14 g
1 oz	28 g
$1^1/_2$ oz	43 g
2 oz	57 g
$2^1/_2$ oz	71 g
3 oz	85 g
$3^1/_2$ oz	100 g
4 oz	113 g
5 oz	142 g
6 oz	170 g
7 oz	200 g
8 oz	227 g
9 oz	255 g
10 oz	284 g
11 oz	312 g
12 oz	340 g
13 oz	368 g
14 oz	400 g
15 oz	425 g
1 lb	454 g

Oven Temperatures

°F	Gas Mark	°C
250	1/2	120
275	1	140
300	2	150
325	3	165
350	4	180
375	5	190
400	6	200
425	7	220
450	8	230
475	9	240
500	10	260
550	Broil	290

Index